Jane Austen's Families

Jane Austen's Families

June Sturrock

ANTHEM PRESS
LONDON · NEW YORK · DELHI

Anthem Press
An imprint of Wimbledon Publishing Company
www.anthempress.com

This edition first published in UK and USA 2014
by ANTHEM PRESS
75–76 Blackfriars Road, London SE1 8HA, UK
or PO Box 9779, London SW19 7ZG, UK
and
244 Madison Ave. #116, New York, NY 10016, USA

First published in hardback by Anthem Press in 2013

Copyright © June Sturrock 2014

The author asserts the moral right to be identified as the author of this work.

All rights reserved. Without limiting the rights under copyright reserved above, no part of this publication may be reproduced, stored or introduced into a retrieval system, or transmitted, in any form or by any means (electronic, mechanical, photocopying, recording or otherwise), without the prior written permission of both the copyright owner and the above publisher of this book.

British Library Cataloguing-in-Publication Data
A catalogue record for this book is available from the British Library.

Library of Congress Cataloging-in-Publication Data
The Library of Congress has catalogued the hardcover edition as follows:
Sturrock, June.
Jane Austen's families / June Sturrock.
pages cm
Includes bibliographical references and index.
ISBN 978-0-85728-296-5 – ISBN 0-85728-296-4
1. Austen, Jane, 1775–1817–Criticism and interpretation. 2. Families in literature. I. Title.
PR4038.F35S78 2013
823'.7–dc23
2012047151

ISBN-13: 978 1 78308 326 8 (Pbk)
ISBN-10: 1 78308 326 3 (Pbk)

This title is also available as an ebook.

For Alan Rudrum

TABLE OF CONTENTS

Acknowledgements	ix
References and Abbreviations	xi
General Introduction	1

Part I Family Dynamics

Introduction		11
Chapter One	The Functions of the Dysfunctional Family: *Northanger Abbey*, *Sense and Sensibility*, *Pride and Prejudice*	15
Chapter Two	Spoilt Children: *Pride and Prejudice*, *Mansfield Park* and *Emma*	33
Chapter Three	"Usefulness and Exertion": Mothers and Sisters in *Sense and Sensibility*, *Mansfield Park*, *Emma* and *Persuasion*	47

Part II Fathers and Daughters

Introduction		67
Chapter Four	Money, Morals and *Mansfield Park*	71
Chapter Five	Speech and Silence in *Emma*	85
Chapter Six	Dandies and Beauties: The Issue of Good Looks in *Persuasion*	99
Conclusion	"Creative Attention"	111

Notes	119
Select Bibliography	135
Index	145

ACKNOWLEDGEMENTS

Shorter and less complex versions of Chapters Three and Five appeared in *Persuasions: The Jane Austen Journal*, "Money, Morals, and *Mansfield Park*: The West Indies Revisited" appeared in *Persuasions* 28 (2006): 176–84 and "Dandies, Beauties, and the Issue of Good Looks in *Persuasion*" appeared in *Persuasions* 26 (2004): 41–50, while Chapter Four is based on an entry in the 2006 *Persuasions On-Line* ("'I am Rather a Talker': Speech and Silence in *Emma*" 28). I am most grateful to Susan Allen Ford, the editor of the journals, and the Jane Austen Society of North America for permissions and for encouragement. Thanks are due to Jocelyn Harris, Diane McColley, Jack Martin and Alan Rudrum for reading parts of this book at various stages. Alan Rudrum, indeed, has read it all more than once and his comments, encouragement and love have meant more to me than I can readily express. I am grateful to the Jane Austen Society of North America, and to the various local chapters of the society at which I have presented talks and papers over the years. Special thanks are due to Keiko Parker. I have learnt much from the various graduate and undergraduate students in Austen classes over the years. I am especially grateful to Dr Corinna Wagner, now of the University of Exeter. I should thank the staffs of the British Library, the Huntington Library, California and Simon Fraser University Library. Any Austen critic writing in the early twenty-first century is indebted to the wealth of previous scholarship and discussion. I hope I have fully acknowledged all these debts in the text and in notes. While thinking about Jane Austen's families I have been very conscious of my own great good fortune as daughter, mother, grandmother, sister, niece and aunt.

REFERENCES AND ABBREVIATIONS

All references are given in parenthesis after quotations and refer to works cited in the Select Bibliography. Where the author has more than one item in the bibliography an abbreviated form of the title is added to the page number. Abbreviations of Jane Austen's novels are as follows: *NA* (*Northanger Abbey*); *S&S* (*Sense and Sensibility*); *P&P* (*Pride and Prejudice*); *MP* (*Mansfield Park*); *E* (*Emma*); *P* (*Persuasion*).

GENERAL INTRODUCTION

Jane Austen's families are not, for my purpose, the Austens, the Austen-Leighs, the Leigh Perrots, or the Knights – actual historical families. My concern is with the Bennets, the Dashwoods, the Bertrams – with the many fictional families whose dynamics are crucial both to Jane Austen's plots and to her explorations of ethical complexities. Most Austen criticism tends to direct its attention to the interactions of the lovers in the various novels. Given Austen's narratives, this concern is inescapable: the relations between Elizabeth and Darcy and between Emma and Mr Knightley, for instance, are crucial to my arguments at various points in this book. Yet my principal interest is the central characters in interaction with their own families and (to a lesser extent) with other family groups, interactions that both foster and retard emotional and moral development.

Significantly, Austen chooses not to write about orphaned heroines,[1] in this respect contrasting strongly with her contemporaries, Frances Burney (Evelina, Camilla, Cecilia), Ann Radcliffe (Emily St Aubert) and Maria Edgeworth (Belinda), and her successors, Charlotte Brontë (Jane Eyre, Shirley Keeldar, Caroline Helstone, Lucy Snowe), George Eliot (Dorothea Brooke, Dinah Morris, Hetty Sorrel) and so on.[2] "Orphan" narratives are convenient enough for many novelists, allowing a protagonist to experience the shocks of the world without the usual parental buffers, but for a writer such as Austen, who cares intensely for what is natural, possible and probable in fiction,[3] the most common early experience of surviving the pains and pleasures of family life provides far richer material. When Walter Scott writes of her ability to communicate "the current of ordinary life" (59) he is surely referring largely to her treatment of family life.

This study includes discussions of the various family interactions in Austen's novels, both intergenerational and intragenerational. Jane Austen writes often of the power and complexity of the love between siblings, which, according to the narrator of *Mansfield Park*, while it is "sometimes almost everything" can also be "worse than nothing" (*MP* 247). At an early stage in all her novels the capacity for affection that is an essential part of the moral nature of all her protagonists shows itself through the love of a brother or sister,[4] and sibling relations, especially between sisters, are an important element in the moral growth of several of her heroines, Marianne Dashwood being merely the most obvious example. Even more significant are the relations between parent and child, and I discuss the ways, both negative and positive, in which Austen's heroines are their parents' daughters – how they respond to and resist their upbringing. Inevitably this concern involves a consideration of the ethics of parenthood and also the ethics these heroines acquire from their parents, through adaptation, imitation and resistance to what they are taught, directly and indirectly. Interactions between parent and child affect both the child in herself and in her active moral life – both what S. L. Goldberg calls "life-morals and conduct morals" (38–9). While Austen's marriage plots depend on the relations between men and women, she is also deeply interested in intergenerational responsibilities, especially in the obligations of the older generation towards the young.

All the same, Austen's novels are never precisely ethically prescriptive. She does not share much of her period's taste for the didactic. In the final words of *Northanger Abbey* she mocks narratives that provide (and readers who expect) simplistic morals: "I leave it to be settled by whomsoever it may concern, whether the tendency of this work may be to recommend parental tyranny, or to reward filial disobedience."[5] As Bharat Tandon says, Austen does not indulge in "the detachable, didactic *sententiae* of which some of her contemporaries were fond" (*Jane Austen* 34). Most notable among such contemporaries was Hannah More, whose *Coelebs in Search of a Wife* (1808) was the best-selling novel of the early nineteenth century.[6] *Coelebs* is structured as a quest for the perfect woman, an unfallen Eve. Coelebs rejects various candidates for his hand for such faults as vanity, coarse manners, over-valuing of accomplishments or wealth, and eventually finds the paragon he has been seeking. The contrast with Austen is clear enough: she does not deal either with paragons or with those who aspire to marry them. While it is certainly possible to provide an itemized list of Austenian virtues (intelligence, charity, self-knowledge), such a list would be both misleading (over-generalized) and less than interesting. In Austen's fiction moral life is dynamic and not static as it is in *Coelebs*. It is complex rather than simple; a matter of responding to precisely imagined situations rather than of acting out absolutes.[7] The significance of self-examination in these novels – Marianne Dashwood's, Darcy's, Elizabeth Bennet's, Sir Thomas Bertram's, for instance – indicates Austen's concept of moral development as an ongoing process. As Alasdair MacIntyre says, "self-knowledge is for Jane Austen both an intellectual and a moral virtue" (241). It is also a virtue most easily acquired in a family, where people often know each other best and comment on each other most freely.

***

Wayne Booth writes that when he began his own work of explicitly ethical criticism, *The Company We Keep*, which was eventually published in 1988, he thought such criticism was unfashionable, but adds that during the process of writing it, he came to the conclusion that "we can no longer pretend that ethical criticism is passé" (19). The philosopher Martha Nussbaum has also written of a (past) period of literary criticism in which "it was assumed that any work that attempts to ask of a literary text questions about how we might live, treating the work as addressed to the reader's practical interests and needs, and as being in some sense about our lives, must be hopelessly naïve, reactionary, and insensitive to the complexities of literary form and intertextual referentiality" (*Love's Knowledge* 21). David Parker comments similarly, noting in 1998 that in "advanced literary circles for most of the 1970s and 1980s, few topics could have been more uninteresting, more depassé, less likely to attract budding young theorists, than the topic 'Ethics and Literature'" ("Introduction" 1). Now, as Sarah Emsley writes, "literary theory has begun to focus on ethics, and moral philosophy has begun to turn to literature in order to illuminate what has been called 'virtue ethics'" (4). Certainly Austen's present-day critics include many like myself who, one way or another, follow the long tradition examining what F. R. Leavis long ago described as Austen's "intense moral interest" (7).[8]

Nussbaum describes the novel as "the central morally serious yet popularly engaging fictional form of our culture" (*Poetic Justice* 6), enlarging on this assertion by arguing that "novels, as a genre, direct us to attend to the concrete; they display before us a wealth of richly realized detail, presented as relevant for choice" (*Poetic Justice* 5). She presents this concern with the concrete in terms of Aristotelian ethics. Robert Miles comments on the same feature of the novel, that is, its specificity about character and situation, and the relation of the specificity to the presentation of the ethical. Miles, however, places this phenomenon in relation to the thought of Kant rather than that of Aristotle:

> The novel imagines the social realities, which ultimately must condition Kant's ethical suppositions, more thoroughly than philosophical speculation invites. According to [Richard] Rorty, it is in the work of Jane Austen that the novel comes into its own as a form capable of refining upon Kant's ethics [...] It is not simply the case that Austen imagines more hypothetical situations in greater detail than a Kantian moral philosopher might do. The difference rather is in the quality of the imagining. (22)[9]

Whether this feature is considered from Kantian or Aristotelian perspectives, it is the ethical implications of such specificity that are relevant here. It is significant that Iris Murdoch, whose literary criticism is nourished by her work both as philosopher and novelist, believes passionately in the importance of the contingent (which implies the concrete, the specific) in the novel: "a respect for the contingent is essential to imagination as opposed to fantasy" ("Against Dryness" 294).[10] As Nussbaum, Miles and Murdoch all show, the novel has ethical value because it presents moral actions within precise contexts, just as they occur in individual lives. Tolstoy knows that we will understand Natasha's destructive infatuation with Anatole Kuragin because he has placed it in two contexts: in the complex human context of Natasha's own youth and vitality, her mother's absence and her father's weakness, her long separation from Prince Andrei, the hostility of his father and sister, Anatole's unscrupulousness and the machinations of the vicious Hélène Bezuhov; and in the highly artificial cultural context of Moscow's operas and parties. Similarly, with Austen, we know precisely why Emma succumbs to the temptation to be witty at Miss Bates's expense – the heat, the general dullness and underlying hostilities at Box Hill, as well as Emma's habitual over-confidence and lack of respect. We also know precisely why, given the different circumstances of the two women, the witticism is an act of cruelty. As Tobin Siebers writes, "to hear all the particulars is to hear […] the kind of story that Jane Austen is in the process of writing" (150).[11]

For Austen, the potential of the novel as a genre was both ethical and artistic. Mary Waldron argues that Austen treats the novel as "primarily an experiment in new possibilities in fiction rather than the vehicle for any moral or didactic purpose" (60).[12] Undoubtedly Austen did recognize and exploit with relish the capacities and conventions of her chosen genre. However, her experiments with the possibilities of fiction, her new standards of "Nature and Probability" (*Letters* 234), in fact allow her to take a new approach to the exploration of ethics in fiction, to represent people as responding to imaginable and complex situations, to show, for instance, Sir Thomas Bertram acting on an uncomfortable mixture of conflicting urges – his duty to save his daughter from an unhappy marriage, his wish to escape social embarrassment and his desire for a rich and powerful new connection. To return to the comparison with Hannah More: More disliked the novel.[13] She saw it as a corrupter of youth, and, like her friend Samuel Johnson, distrusted "mixed characters."[14] Her natural bent was for the didactic poem or essay, for the elegantly balanced generalization and for intelligent moralizing. She neither could nor would exploit what would become the real ethical strength of the novel: its potential for showing morality in action in concrete situations. Austen, relishing the novel, an expert in all its achievements and idiocies from an early age, as her juvenilia show, used all of its potential for entertainment and for ethical explorations. Even Austen's artistic economy has an ethical bent: nothing is wasted, everything tells, either on the development of her narrative or on its implications.

* * *

As my own understanding of the ethical necessarily affects my reading of Austen, I should attempt to clarify my position briefly. In my ideas of the good I am indebted to Murdoch's concept of "attention," a word she uses "to express the idea of a just and loving gaze directed upon an individual reality" – the reality of a person, that is. She goes on: "I believe this to be the characteristic and proper mark of the active moral agent" ("Idea" 327). For Murdoch, attention involves the attempt "to see justly, to overcome prejudice, to avoid temptation, to control and curb imagination, to direct reflection" so that in our relations with other people we perceive people, as far as possible, as they are and not as we imagine them or fantasize about them for the purposes of our own psychological comfort ("Idea" 332). For Murdoch, therefore, the moral life is not a matter of discrete decisions but an unending intellectual process, "something that goes on continually, not something that is switched off in between the occurrence of specific moral choices" ("Idea" 329).

Murdoch borrows (and adapts) this concept from Simone Weil, who defines attention as the act of "suspending our thought, leaving it detached, empty and ready to be penetrated by the object" (*Waiting on God* 72).[15] Weil is concerned with attention as what removes the mind from its habitual solipsistic preoccupations and anxieties, and focuses it on the Other – for Weil above all on God: "attention taken to its highest degree, is the same thing as prayer" (*Gravity and Grace* 105). But she also believes that "love for our neighbour" is "made of creative attention" (*Waiting on God* 105). Murdoch, of course, removes Weil's concept from the religious realm and uses it in relation to secular ethics.

Murdoch's concept of attention has been applied to the discussion of aesthetics. Elaine Scarry, whose concern in *On Beauty and Being Just* is the interaction between aesthetics and ethics, uses the related ideas of Murdoch and Weil to explore the idea of the beautiful as compelling "attention" to the significance of what is beyond the self, in what she calls a "radical decentering" (111–14). Scarry's idea of decentering, though, is a response to an external stimulus rather than an internal habit: it deals, so to speak, with Fanny Price admiring the stars, rather than with Fanny Price trying to be fair to Mary Crawford – though Scarry would perhaps argue that Fanny's openness to the starry night, to Cowper's poetry, even to the evergreens in the Parsonage shrubbery, prepares her to be open to the needs of her rival.

More specifically, several writers have applied Murdoch's idea of "attention" to literary issues; after all, it was Murdoch, "more than any other figure of her generation," as Martha Nussbaum claims, who "challenged us to think better about the moral significance of the imagination" ("Faint" 137). As Simon Haines shows, Murdoch herself writes of literature "as being something between an 'analogy' and a 'case' of moral thought. And reading it, taking it seriously, criticizing it, is therefore also a mode of ethical reflection [...]

'the most educational of all human activities'" (30). Nussbaum acknowledges the relation of her own thoughts on the importance of imaginative work to that of Murdoch (*Love's Knowledge* 143).[16] She also writes, in terms that recall Murdoch's idea of "attention," of

> an ethical ability that I call "perception," after both Aristotle and [Henry] James. By this I mean the ability to discern, acutely and responsively, the salient features of one's particular situation. The Aristotelian conception argues that this ability is at the core of what practical wisdom is, and that it is not only a tool toward achieving the correct action or statement but an ethically valuable activity in its own right. (*Love's Knowledge* 37)

Murdoch's concept of attention speaks of a concentration on the actuality of other people rather than "a particular situation," but the relation between the two "ethical abilities" is clear. For Nussbaum, as for Murdoch, literature can refine or activate this ability: "By cultivating our ability to see vividly another person's distress, to picture ourselves in another person's place [...] we make ourselves more likely to respond with the morally illuminating and appropriate sort of response" (*Love's Knowledge* 339).[17]

"Attention," "perception" or a degree of "radical decentering" – all these terms might describe that quality we see in Mr Knightley, who perceives Harriet's embarrassment and humiliation at the Ball at the Crown Inn and does something about it, who notices that Jane Fairfax is singing herself hoarse and does something about it. As Stuart Tave says, "the effect of Mr Knightley's imagination is not to make him build a private world of his own feelings but to turn himself outward to a delicate understanding of what lies beyond himself, in the feelings of others" (235). This quality is what develops within Fanny Price at Portsmouth, as she perceives Susan's distress over her silver knife and, more generally, her own ignorance. Fanny, liberated by a little experience and a little money, acts on both these perceptions despite her extreme diffidence. Anne Elliot's behaviour throughout *Persuasion*, to Mary and her children, to all the Musgroves, to Mrs Smith, to Captain Benwick, demonstrates her exceptional capacity for attention. Like Fanny Price, though, Anne has to learn to act on her own desires as well as those of other people. What Emma fails in, as an "imaginist," is attention to the actuality of most other people. Similarly, Marianne Dashwood has to open her eyes to the claims of those she has formerly dismissed as unthinkably vulgar or unintelligent, and thus not worth consideration. Robert Miles directs his attention to those characters of Austen who do not change:

> When we are told that Aunt Norris talks '*at*' rather than to Fanny, she stands convicted of immorality: the immorality of denying the otherness

of others. Mr Woodhouse is similarly immoral, in that he cannot imagine that others see things differently from the way he does, although this failing is treated in a less harsh – in a generally more comic – fashion. (15 – emphasis in the original)[18]

In fact, much of Austen's comedy is based on the failure of attention: the conversation between Mr Weston and Mrs Elton at the Woodhouses' dinner-party provides high comedy because neither devotes the least attention to the other. Similarly the interactions between Admiral Croft and Sir Walter Elliot are funny because neither has the slightest idea of the other's sensations. Emma and Marianne change through a self-examination, which is different from self-absorption. To think beyond the self, then, to "pay attention" is to be "morally active" (Murdoch "Idea" 314).

* * *

The following discussions of Austen's novels address the ethical implications of various family interactions in the novels through close examination. James Thompson argues that, as critics, we need to see Austen's work "as explicitly time-bound and historical, not the product of right or truth or nature or even a powerful morality" (6). Thompson's position comes from a sense of the difficulty that arises both from the familiarity of Austen's work and from a critical tendency to begin by "sharing their [Austen's novels] assumptions" (6). The difficulty is real: I am certainly aware that while I tend to read nineteenth-century domestic fiction (Charlotte Yonge, Margaret Oliphant) out of a sense of curiosity as to what it *was* like, I tend to read Austen from a position that is, critically, equally impracticable, that is, out of a sense of curiosity as to what it *is* like. The first "it," I suppose, refers to Victorian social life and assumptions, the second to life in general, whatever that may be. The different temptations in reading these novelists indicate a different understanding of the nature of these texts. There is a tendency to read Austen as universal and general, as writing about life itself. Yet it is possible, perhaps inevitable, for the historical critic both to perceive a text as time-bound and to perceive the ways in which it does and does not reach across time, perhaps towards a moral vision or a moral process that twenty-first century readers can understand as well, though in some ways differently than their predecessors. That is how we read.

Linda Hutcheon claims that all adaptations in whatever genre are "palimpsestuous," so that the informed audience is conscious of the original work beneath the adaptation (6). In a sense all historically informed readings present a similar palimpsest in that we see the text with double vision, dimly conscious of a possible early nineteenth-century reading under our twenty-first century reading.[19] This kind of historical double vision is perhaps what Karl Kroeber has in mind when he writes of Austen:

> Her fiction enables us to discriminate underlying principles of personal relations. This is why, like so many fine novelists, she will appear to some readers "immoral." Her ethics cannot be comprehended within the prevailing code of conduct of her time. But because she uncovers ideal possibilities of relationship beneath specialized manifestations constituting a particular etiquette, her fiction persists as means for judging all kinds of manners, including those (inconceivable to her) of our time. (151)

***

The following discussions of family relations in Austen's novels are divided into two parts, each of which is prefaced by a brief introduction. Part I, "Family Dynamics," includes discussions of specific kinds of family interactions in various groups of novels. In Chapter One, I examine the role of the dysfunctional family in the three Steventon novels, *Northanger Abbey*, *Sense and Sensibility* and *Pride and Prejudice*, in terms both of plot and of ethical implications. Chapter 2 discusses a theme repeated throughout Austen's work, that of the spoilt child, focusing on *Pride and Prejudice*, *Mansfield Park* and *Emma*. Chapter Three focuses on the role of the mother in Austen's fiction, examining both how the mother influences the relations between her daughters and how she influences the daughters' ideas of their traditional domestic responsibilities. In Part II, I focus on the contrast between daughters and fathers or father-figures in the three Chawton novels, commenting on how the contrast between parent and child is displayed in a central trope of each of these novels, money in the case of *Mansfield Park*, speech in *Emma* and the question of personal appearance in *Persuasion*.

Part I

FAMILY DYNAMICS

INTRODUCTION

> The parents in Miss Austen's novels are less like savage wild beasts than those of her predecessors, but she evidently looks upon them with suspicion, and an uneasy feeling that *le père de famille est capable de tout* makes itself sufficiently apparent throughout the greater part of her writings.

These words of Samuel Butler, writing in *The Way of All Flesh*,[1] certainly exaggerate, for none of Austen's *pères de famille* approaches Butler's own Mr Pontifex in savagery. All the same, they are based on the perfectly accurate perception that Austen refuses to idealize her families. Parents and children alike have their own personal preoccupations, their strengths and weaknesses, as well as their responsibilities. The ideal is not readily combined with the particular and Austen is concerned as a novelist with the particular. Through particular actions and interactions – through the Eltons laughing together at Mr Elton's refusal to dance with Harriet or through Fanny Price uncomplainingly cutting roses under a midsummer sun – she establishes the moral world of her characters.

Austen's heroines develop partly because of and partly in spite of the faults and foibles of the families from which they emerge. Moral sense, after all, must involve some knowledge of and contact with evil. Unlike many of her successors and admirers, such as Henry James, Elizabeth Bowen, Iris Murdoch or Penelope Fitzgerald, Austen was not particularly interested in the question of innocence as such. Her only "innocent" heroine is Catherine Morland: all of the others are acutely aware of some of the faults and failings in others. Catherine accordingly must learn about evil from other families as her own fails to provide such experience directly. The first chapter, "The Functions of the Dysfunctional Family," looks at the three novels written at Steventon and the literary necessity of the family flaws of Morlands, Thorpes, Tilneys, Dashwoods and Bennets, both in terms of plot development and in terms of the various heroines' maturation. The second chapter, "Spoilt Children," examines a parental failing common to all Austen's novels and its varied effects on its victims, looking especially at Mr Darcy, Maria Bertram and Emma Woodhouse. The discussion of the maternal role in "Usefulness and Exertion," the third chapter, shows the strong influence of the mother, whether living or dead, focusing on *Sense and Sensibility*, *Mansfield Park*, *Emma* and *Persuasion*. Relations between siblings, especially between sisters, affect the moral life of Austen's heroines: this chapter shows how these relations respond to the mother's character and actions, which also help form the daughters' sense of their traditional domestic role, a moral concern in the work of a novelist so concerned with the value of exertion.

Austen was evidently fascinated by family dynamics, by the constant negotiation between one's own claims and those of other people demanded by family life. This fascination interacts with what Claudia Johnson calls Austen's "scepticism about the family" (*Jane Austen* 72), her refusal to romanticize an institution that has often, and damagingly, been treated as sacred both in her own times and in ours. In a caustic commentary on her treatment of parent-child relations, Christopher Ricks writes that she was great

> because she did not minister to the over-estimation of parental and filial love. To which might be added a different, though not contradictory admonition; not that such love is less important than we have got into the way of believing, or pretending to believe, but insofar as such love is truly important, it is far less imaginable – less sharable – than we have allowed ourselves to permit. (94)

So in the same way that she leaves her love scenes almost entirely to the imaginations of her readers, she rarely emphasizes the love between parent and child. The poignancy of such passages as those showing Mr Bennet's concern that Elizabeth should not experience married unhappiness like his or the exaggerated feeling shown by Emma weeping over the idea of leaving her father as "a sin of thought" (369) are all the more telling. What Austen is more usually concerned with are the common interactions of everyday domestic life.

A common pattern in women's fiction of the later eighteenth and early nineteenth century is that of Maria Edgeworth's Belinda or Ann Radcliffe's Emily, of the orphaned young woman facing the challenges of the world alone. However, Jane Austen is certainly not alone among her contemporaries in her interest in family relations and the effects of these relations on her heroines. For instance, Amelia Opie's two best-known novels bear the titles *The Father and Daughter* (1801) and *Adeline Mowbray: or, The Mother and Daughter* (1804), and in the latter the theme of the harm done by foolish parenting extends over three generations: the heroine's unhappiness is a result of her mother's selfishness and folly, which is in turn the result of parental spoiling. Like Opie,

Austen is well aware of the moral obligations of parents to their children and of the possible damage done by parental failure. However, whereas Opie represents the adverse consequences of faulty parenting as being virtually automatic, Austen's representations of the family are less pessimistic – and perhaps more realistic. Parental faults or limitations affect every one of Austen's heroines but Austen shows them as refusing to be determined by the dysfunctionality of others and as developing into happy women.

Chapter One

THE FUNCTIONS OF THE DYSFUNCTIONAL FAMILY: *NORTHANGER ABBEY, SENSE AND SENSIBILITY, PRIDE AND PREJUDICE*

Without Satan, Paradise is not Lost and English poetry loses its great epic. Without malevolence or folly, knaves or fools, no narrative is possible. And in many narratives the encounter with folly or malevolence leads to enlightenment: Nietzsche writes that the wisdom of Oedipus and the understanding of Hamlet are bought by unnatural acts.[1] In Jane Austen's fiction virtually every character and situation is affected by the flaws and contradictions on which narrative depends. When she proclaims that "pictures of perfection make me sick & wicked" (*Letters* 335), she writes, then, both as novelist and critic. Austen's own critics and admirers have often quoted these words; they provide the epigraph of Mary Waldron's *Jane Austen and the Fiction of her Time* and the title of Reginald Hill's clever detective story, *Pictures of Perfection*.[2] There is good reason for such reiteration. None of her heroines is a picture of perfection in the mode of Hannah More's Lucilla,[3] though Austen felt at one time that Anne Elliot – "almost too good for me" – came perilously near it (*Letters* 335) and though some critics have quite mistakenly assumed that she intended poor little Fanny Price as an epitome of the Evangelical virtues.[4]

The families that produce these young women and their friends, rivals and suitors are equally mixed. Austen certainly represents happy families but none of those families is treated so unrealistically as to be flawless. The Morlands' affection and good sense provide Catherine with strong principles, but the lack of imagination of these "plain matter-of-fact people" (*NA* 86) prepares neither Catherine nor her brother James adequately for contact with other families with different codes of conduct. The Dashwood family is close and shares strong intellectual interests but the mother's indulgence of feeling at the expense of prudence harms her daughters and especially the favourite daughter who resembles her so closely. The Darcys are loving and intelligent but too exclusive. The Woodhouses support each other affectionately but suffer from their intellectual inequalities. The Musgroves are warm, "friendly and hospitable," but "not much educated" (*P* 78) and so undemanding of their children that the heir to the estate ends up idle and unambitious, though amiable. However, while no Austen family functions perfectly, some obviously manage better than others. This chapter explores Austen's use of the less happy families.

As a convenience, I use the sociologists' word "dysfunctional" (rather loosely) to describe those families whose interactions either harm the younger generation morally or cause the younger generation exceptional pain.[5] All plot development in Austen's six novels depends to some extent on such adverse interactions, as they show young women of principle learning to negotiate an imperfect world while retaining, or in some cases fully realizing, these principles. In the three Steventon novels in particular, *Northanger Abbey*, *Sense and Sensibility* and *Pride and Prejudice*, the role of the less-than-perfect family is important to narrative as well as to moral development. In *Northanger Abbey*, the novel's narrative depends on the heroine's departure from her tranquil home and her encounters with two dysfunctional families. In *Pride and Prejudice* it is the dysfunctionality of the heroine's own family that moves the plot along, while *Sense and Sensibility*, with its two heroines, combines both processes, its narrative impelled by faults both within and beyond its central family.

* * *

Northanger Abbey is commonly described as a novel dealing with a girl's introduction to the world, in the vein of Burney's *Evelina* or Edgeworth's *Belinda*, or a dozen other novels*:* "As in so many works of the period, an inexperienced girl is on the threshold of life," writes Marilyn Butler (170).[6] Catherine Morland's naïveté and innocence at the beginning of the novel are partly the result of her youth – she is only seventeen – but they are intensified by her life in the small village of Fullerton as a member of a large, tranquil and affectionate clerical family. Her circumstances cushion her. Moreover, Austen carefully normalizes the Morland family. Their behaviour shows "a degree of *moderation* and composure […] consistent with the *common* feelings of *common* life" (44 – my emphases).[7] Catherine, too, is normalized: all the playful references in the first chapter to her status as a heroine establish that having been an ordinary little girl, she has become an ordinary young woman. Her family life can be seen, as Mary Waldron sees it, as "superficially ideal, but in practice unhelpful" (28). It is, perhaps, both helpful and unhelpful, in that Catherine acquires principles but lacks experience. Certainly it is hardly surprising that she expects the world to be as safe and comfortable as Fullerton Rectory, when she sets out for Bath, "free from the apprehension of evil as from the knowledge of it" (227).[8] She is not able initially to recognize behaviour that falls below her own "'innate principle of general integrity,'" as Henry Tilney describes it (212), unless that behaviour is dressed up in the extremes of Gothic convention. Her limited experience and under-exercised imagination guide her expectations. She is, as Juliet McMaster points out, "anchored in her own practice and unawakened to other people's. As Tilney tells her, 'with you it is not, How is such a one likely to be influenced? [...] but, how should I be influenced'" (*Novelist* 210). In order to function as an adult woman, Catherine needs a more complex understanding of human society, and Bath begins to provide this, with its introductions to the Tilneys and the Thorpes.[9] Both these single-parent families suffer in various ways through parental failures, the Tilneys through an over-controlling father and the Thorpes through an over-indulgent mother.

The plot of the first volume of *Northanger Abbey* depends largely on Isabella and John Thorpe and the blindness of both Catherine and her brother James to their lies, their silliness, their boastfulness and their mercenary attitude towards courtship. Austen implicitly connects the follies and manoeuvres of John and Isabella to the behaviour of their widowed mother, "a good-humoured, well-meaning woman, and a very indulgent mother" (57) – "'too indulgent,'" according to Mr Allen (119). To mean well is proverbially not enough. Mrs Thorpe's maternal blindness to her children's faults and her too easy compliance with all their wishes result in spite and jealousy within her family as well as the predatory aggressions of John and Isabella beyond their family. Catherine – apparently more perceptive than her older brother – is only briefly deceived by the boring and loutish John Thorpe, but for both the young Morlands Isabella's beauty and flattery are too pleasant to invite immediate analysis.[10]

Catherine's adult development begins with her connection with this dysfunctional family. The extent of her development should not be exaggerated, however.[11] At the end of the novel she is very much the frank and affectionate young woman that she was at the beginning. J. F. Burrows, in his study of idiolect in Austen, comments that, of all the characters whose speech he examined, "Catherine and Mrs Elton show least change in their idiolects as the novels unfold" (136), and, given Austen's extraordinary capacity to communicate character and its changes through speech, this limited change indicates that Catherine is still in the process of maturing at the end of the novel (when indeed she is only eighteen). However, Marilyn Butler's assertion that she learns little in the first volume of *Northanger Abbey* (176) is over-emphatic, as Catherine has, in fact, begun slowly to acquire some discernment and discrimination. By the time she leaves Bath for Northanger, she has learnt to discard any belief she may have had in the sincerity of John Thorpe's attachment to her, and although she does not entirely suspect Isabella of being untrue to her engagement to James, Catherine is concerned enough to watch

Isabella closely both with James and with his wealthier rival, Captain Tilney, and to ask Henry Tilney to speak to his brother. And later, when Isabella, disappointed of Captain Tilney, attempts to use Catherine as a go-between to patch up her engagement to James, Catherine has learnt enough to recognize instantly the "inconsistencies, contradiction, and falsehood" of her letter and to refuse to answer it (211).

In the second volume, Austen's focus shifts from Bath to Northanger and from the Thorpes to the Tilneys. The contrast between the two families is obvious enough, and Butler argues that "the arrangement of the two pairs of brothers and sisters, the Tilneys and the Thorpes, virtually forces the reader into a series of ethical comparisons between them on the author's terms" (178). However, Austen's use of the conjunction of the two families is by no means as crudely and dogmatically presented as Butler seems to suggest. Certainly she provides a moral contrast between the two sets of siblings, but that contrast is too obvious to warrant much examination. Eleanor and Henry Tilney are evidently polite, scrupulous and intelligent, with intellectual interests, whereas the Thorpes have none of these qualities. However, Austen also indicates a matter of far greater interest – the parallel between the two families. The Tilney children suffer emotionally as the children of a widowed father who overexerts his parental authority and the Thorpes suffer morally as the children of a widowed mother who fails to exert any authority. Moreover, the rich widower's defects echo those of the children of the impecunious widow. The freedoms given by money and social position have apparently the same power to corrupt as the freedoms given by an over-indulgent upbringing. Certainly the General, like Isabella and John Thorpe, is mercenary and manipulative. Like them, he uses language to mislead, to flatter, to enhance his own importance and to advance his family's financial position, and like them he underestimates other people's principles.

Catherine suffers through her interaction with these families, undergoing more distress at Northanger because of her greater involvement with the young Tilneys and because General Tilney has more power to behave badly than the young Thorpes. The learning that comes about through this suffering is part of Catherine's development into an adult ready for "perfect happiness at the [age] of […] eighteen" (239). Austen shows the intellectual growth of Catherine as involving the understanding that the young and the middle-aged, the wealthy and the not-so-wealthy, men and women – all are potentially exploiters. She learns, too, that human speech, like human behaviour, is more complex and more suspect in the world beyond Fullerton. The most obvious similarity between General Tilney, Isabella Thorpe and John Thorpe, is their misuse of language, through flattery, exaggeration and downright lies.

The socialization of Catherine is very much involved in her developing sense of the possibilities and pitfalls of language. In *Northanger Abbey*, as later in *Emma*, Austen insists on the importance of language: spoken language through the combination of fantasy and pedantry in the speech of Henry Tilney as well as through the falsifications already mentioned;[12] written language through the famous defence of the novel at the end of chapter five, the many conversations about fiction and the Tilneys' discussion with Catherine about historical writing. As with another very young heroine, Fanny Price – and to a greater degree – Catherine's moral education comes partly from her reading. For the more bookish, more intelligent and far more vulnerable Fanny, her reading seems to have contributed to making her at least temporarily priggish, a fault that is surely more excusable in the very young and very sensitive than some critics suppose.[13] Catherine presents a rather different case: instead of Crabbe, Cowper and Macartney, the unintellectual Catherine is consuming Mrs Radcliffe. These novels effectively and usefully introduce her to evil, but only in its most extreme forms, as crime and intrigue. She remains blind to subtleties of conduct. Noticing evil for the first time, she assumes that it must involve serious crime.[14] After all, General Tilney is unpleasant – irritable, embarrassing and dominating, "accustomed on every ordinary occasion to give the law in his family" (236). Catherine's (accurate) perception of him combined with her reading drive her therefore to suspect him of either murdering or hiding away his wife. After all, she has read of "dozens who had persevered in every possible vice, going on from crime to crime, murdering whomsoever they chose, without any feeling of humanity or remorse" (188).[15]

This misjudgement, in that it involves a new readiness to see evil, is a crucial stage in Catherine's moral development, as is her rapid reaction to Henry Tilney's discovery of her suspicions. His immediate grasp of Catherine's misapprehension indicates that he is well aware of his father's failings. All the same, he has already been established as unable to resist any opportunity to teach a young woman a lesson. His humiliating interrogation of Catherine and his ensuing lecture on probability and the behaviour of English families drive Catherine to the understanding, not that she has completely misjudged General Tilney, but that

> among the English [...] there was a general though unequal mixture of good and bad. Upon this conviction, she would not be surprised if even in Henry and Eleanor Tilney, some slight imperfection might hereafter appear; and upon this conviction she need not fear to acknowledge some actual specks in the character of their father, who, though cleared from the grossly injurious suspicions which she must ever blush to have entertained, she did believe, upon serious consideration, to be not perfectly amiable. (196–7)

Catherine discovers the possibility of "imperfection" in her immediate circle and even in those she loves best, Henry and Eleanor. This discovery, so difficult to her unsuspicious and affectionate nature, is made possible by the interaction between her reading and her actual experience of dysfunctional families, Thorpes and Tilneys. The Tilneys, she realizes, are habitually suppressed by a dominating and ill-tempered father, in whose presence they are uncomfortable.[16] The General may, as his son asserts, have valued his wife, but he also gave her "much to bear" (194) through his temper, as he still does the daughter whose life, as the nominal mistress of his house, is one of "patient suffering" and "habitual endurance" (238), and no real power.

Catherine's most painful lesson is naturally the one that affects her personally and directly. When she learns that the General has ordered her to be sent away from Northanger as if in disgrace, she faces directly the reality of evil. Austen compares her condition on her last night at the Abbey with her first night, which she had spent tormenting herself with Radcliffean terrors:

> Yet how different now the source of her inquietude from what it had been then – how mournfully superior in reality and substance! Her anxiety had foundation in fact, her fears in probability; and with a mind so occupied in the contemplation of actual and natural evil, the solitude of her situation, the darkness of her chamber, the antiquity of the building were felt and considered without the smallest emotion. (218)

"Actual and natural evil" provide Catherine with experience that she needs and that Fullerton Rectory could never provide. Robert Miles argues:

> Austen's moral purpose and the achievement of personality in fiction are [...] of a piece. Her characters change according to the company they keep because their inner selves are dynamic. And their inner selves are dynamic because there is a tension between what they feel and what they decide to do; between their desires and the moral codes that direct correct action; between self and other. (15)

Catherine must encounter "actual and natural evil" or become morally stagnant. Both the plot and the moral interest of the second volume of *Northanger Abbey* depend on the Tilneys' dysfunctionality – on the General's avarice, insincerity and bad temper, and his children's unhappiness – just as in the first volume they depended on the falsity of the Thorpes.

***

The Morland family's comfortable cohesiveness and matter-of-factness, as well as the small world they inhabit at Fullerton, where all Catherine can do for entertainment is "go and call on Mrs Allen" (97), mean that she must look outside her normal surroundings for experience and for a "hero" (6). Like Catherine, Elizabeth and Jane Bennet make decidedly exogamous marriages and like her they find for themselves matches that are "under every pecuniary view […] beyond [their] claims" (*NA* 237). However, in contrast to the Morlands, the Bennet family provides its daughters with a thorough education in faults and follies. It is her family's lack of cohesion and comfort that makes Elizabeth happy to leave her home behind for "all the comfort and elegance of [the] family party at Pemberley" (382), while even the more tolerant Jane and Bingley soon prefer to move some distance away from Longbourne.

The Bennet family's failure to provide proper mutual support is crucial to the plot of *Pride and Prejudice*. As Julia Prewitt Brown comments, "the moral centre of [*Pride and Prejudice*] lies in the connection between the parent generation and the present generation" (*Jane Austen's Novels* 8). The embarrassing behaviour of their parents and sisters, by driving away Bingley and by fostering in Darcy the proud distaste that helps to make his first proposal to Elizabeth so (literally unacceptably) rude and arrogant, delays the marriages of Jane and Elizabeth long enough to provide the novel with the necessary narrative impetus.

The elder Bennets' failings as individuals and more especially as parents and as spouses are apparent throughout the novel. These faults become, of course, most publicly and embarrassingly evident at the Netherfield Ball, an episode in which the comedy is acutely painful both to Elizabeth and to the reader. At the ball, Mrs Bennet speaks loudly and without shame of her designs on Bingley, Mr Bennet restrains Mary too unkindly and too publicly, Mary displays her lack both of musicianship and of proper modesty, and Mr Collins inevitably makes a fool of himself and his family. These failings, "that total want of propriety so frequently, so almost uniformly betrayed by [Mrs Bennet], by [Elizabeth's] three younger sisters, and occasionally even by [her] father" (218) are the chief "causes of repugnance" (218) that concern Darcy enough to make him hesitate over Elizabeth and discourage the amenable Bingley from pursuing his courtship of Jane. Elizabeth is forced to realize that "Jane's disappointment had in fact been the work of her nearest relations" (227) – their "folly and indecorum" (231). A further delay in the two principal marriage narratives is the result of Lydia's elopement. Austen directly associates Lydia's behaviour, which leads to her marriage to "one of the most worthless young men in Great Britain" (314) and might well have led to her ending up on the streets, with the complete lack of parental control that results from Mrs Bennet's indulgence and Mr Bennet's inertia. In fact, the whole plot of *Pride and Prejudice* can be seen as dependent on the dysfunctionality of the Bennet family. The 2005 film adaptation of *Pride and Prejudice*, directed by Joe Wright, in sweetening the Bennet marriage and focusing on the Bennets as a loving family, changes both the meaning and the dynamics of Austen's novel.[17] Domestic discomfort fuels the plot of *Pride and Prejudice*.

But it is not in plot alone that *Pride and Prejudice* gains from the family discomforts. The novel is deeply concerned both with the nature of marriage and the obligations of parents. The unsuitable marriage of Mr and Mrs Bennet and the uneasy interactions of the family as a whole are central to both these concerns and especially the discussion of marriage that subtly permeates the novel. If at the end of *Pride and Prejudice* Austen presents Elizabeth and Jane as justified in their expectation of married happiness, in the body of the novel she has certainly demonstrated that such a state is not easily or thoughtlessly achieved. In this, *Pride and Prejudice* resembles *Sense and Sensibility*. The successful marriages of the ending of *Sense and Sensibility* must be seen in the context not only of the unromantic nature of these matches – Elinor's to a man who lacks both looks and charm, Marianne's to a man for whom she feels merely "strong esteem and lively friendship" (380) – but also of the marriages of the ill-assorted Palmers and Middletons, and of the John Dashwoods, who bring out the worst in each other. "Jane Austen's comedy never quite allows the satisfaction of the dreamwork's desires," writes Isobel Armstrong (78), and in *Pride and Prejudice* the "dreamwork's" desire is kept in check by the sense that pervades this novel that marriage is infinitely difficult and debatable. Charlotte Lucas's entire function in the novel seems to be to further the discussion of marriage: she argues with Elizabeth over the importance of knowing one's future spouse well before marriage: "'Happiness in marriage is entirely a matter of chance,'" she avers (61). She herself marries Mr Collins purely for the sake of "a comfortable home" (154), and she manages her own distaste for her "irksome" (152) husband with remarkable competence. Given Charlotte's intelligence, her ideas about marriage cannot be instantly dismissed, and she is shown as happy enough in her domestic responsibilities.

Elizabeth's conversations with Mrs Gardiner also feed into the debate about money and marriage: should Elizabeth encourage the penniless Wickham? Should Wickham court the rich (but freckled) Mary King? "'Pray, my dear aunt, what is the difference in matrimonial affairs, between the mercenary and the prudent motive?'" asks Elizabeth (180). Elizabeth's two rejected proposals address similar concerns. Both Mr Collins and Mr Darcy assume that Elizabeth will happily accept such a favourable position as they offer, while Elizabeth is determined not to marry without respect. This respect she eventually comes to feel for Darcy, as she realizes how happy they might have been together: "It was an union that must have been to the advantage of both: by her ease and liveliness his mind might have been softened, his manners improved, and from his judgement, information, and knowledge of the world, she must have received benefit of greater importance." At this point she concludes gloomily, "but no such happy marriage could now teach the admiring multitude what connubial felicity really was" (318). And connubial felicity, for Elizabeth, is evidently in large part, though certainly not entirely, a matter of intellectual, moral and social exchange.

Austen's representation of the Bennets' marriage is crucial to the discussion of the nature of marriage in *Pride and Prejudice*. One of the most important passages about marriage concerns Elizabeth's feelings about her parents' relationship. The narrator informs us that after a marriage based entirely on sexual attraction, Mr Bennet's "respect, esteem, and confidence" (250) in his wife quickly vanish, reducing her in his eyes to a mere source of amusement for her "ignorance and folly" (250) – as well as, presumably, a sexual partner.[18] His loss of respect for her seems to involve a loss of respect for himself. Such a loss of respect may be the inevitable result of his choice; but the choice was faulty in itself and his failure to conceal his contempt is a much less excusable fault, involving as it does a degree of cruelty to her and indifference to the wellbeing of their children. Elizabeth recognizes

> the impropriety of her father's behaviour as a husband. She had always seen it with pain; but respecting his abilities, and grateful for his affectionate treatment of herself she endeavoured […] to banish from her thoughts that continual breach of conjugal obligation and decorum, which in exposing his wife to the contempt of her own children, was so reprehensible. (250–51)

Austen implies first that marriage should be based on respect, esteem and confidence, all of which comes about from intellectual equality. Moreover, it demands a "decorum" which precludes making a fool of one's spouse in front of other people, especially one's own children. Mr Bennet's own shame and unhappiness become apparent in one his very few serious speeches, the touching appeal to Elizabeth not to marry without love and respect, which show a similar sense of the requirements of a happy marriage:

> I know your disposition, Lizzy. I know you could neither be happy nor respectable, unless you truly esteemed your husband; unless you looked up to him as a superior. Your lively talents would place you in the greatest danger in an unequal marriage. You could scarcely escape discredit and misery. My child, let me not have the grief of seeing *you* unable to respect your partner in life. You know not what you are about. (375 – Austen's emphasis)

This speech is the only direct indication Austen provides of his unhappiness, and it is all the more touching because it shows his deep affection for Elizabeth. It also shows a similar sense of the requirements for happy marriage – intellectual equality or similarity (Mr Bennet prefers male superiority), esteem, respect – that Elizabeth has already come to see as essential. Love, sexual love, is vital to the narrative but love, properly understood, includes these qualities, which are necessary for a good marriage.[19] Even the charitable Jane is only able to countenance the Lucas/Collins marriage in the hope that Charlotte can feel "something like regard and esteem" (165) for Mr Collins.[20]

If Mr Bennet is unhappy in his marriage, it is unlikely that his wife finds it perfectly fulfilling. Mr Bennet's intellectual habits encourage him to contemplate and analyse the roots of his discomfort. Mrs Bennet has no such resource, so that her sense of unease is expressed in a more dispersed and inarticulate way, through her "poor nerves" (143). John Wiltshire's brief commentary on Mrs Bennet's nerves is illuminating: he describes her as "converting frustration into illness" (*Body* 21). He sees her nervous bouts as "the correlate of her anxiety over her five unmarried daughters," and notes that they become manifest "when both her obsession with their futures has been brought specifically out as an issue, and her powerlessness within the family, the futility of her schemes, has been bluntly reinscribed in her consciousness" (*Body* 20). His arguments are convincing, but surely her (perhaps unconscious) discomfort in her marriage is an equally important source of her "nervous complaints" (144).

Like the nature of marriage, parental obligation and parental failure are recurrent concerns of *Pride and Prejudice*. Darcy comes to realize that his parents, good though they were, "allowed, encouraged, almost taught [him] to be selfish and over-bearing" (368). Lady Catherine De Bourgh's surplus of confidence, energy and willpower have reduced her daughter to a silent and feeble cipher. Mr Collins's natural inadequacies have been made worse by "an illiterate and miserly father" (104). The extravagant Wickham is the son of an extravagant mother. But again, it is the older Bennets, naturally, whose parental faults receive the most careful scrutiny. Their failures as parents are placed in relation to their marital failures, their lack of "conjugal felicity or domestic comfort" in a marriage without "respect, esteem, and confidence" (250). Elizabeth is well aware of "the disadvantages which must attend the children of so unsuitable a marriage" (251).

Austen represents Mrs Bennet's parental weaknesses in a fairly conventional way, as the stuff of comedy. Austen is dealing here with a known trope of the period. Thomas Gisborne, in his *Enquiry into the Duties of the Female Sex* (1797), which Austen seems to have liked,[21] deplores parental "scheming eagerness respecting the settlement of their daughters in marriage" (388) and, more specifically, warns that "the forward advances and studied attentions of the mother to young men of fortune whom she wishes to call her sons-in-law are often in the highest degree distressing to her daughters as well as offensive to the other parties; and in many cases actually prevent attachments, which would otherwise have taken place" (392–3). *Pride and Prejudice* presents a comic enactment of this generalization. Despite the fact that she has made their marriages "the business of her life" (45), as Roger Gard says, "Mrs Bennet's behaviour has almost cost both her older daughters their future husbands" (150). A third daughter is affected by her bungling attempts to marry them all off: Peter Knox-Shaw comments, "it is precisely Mrs Bennet's relentless match-making that seals Lydia's fate by putting her into Wickham's hands, her pandering on this occasion nearly destroying the hopes of her two elder daughters" (9). Given the middle-class mores of the period, she jeopardizes Lydia's marriageability in endangering her respectability.

Various critics have defended Mrs Bennet, noting the economic desirability of marriage for middle-class women, at the period, especially those in the Bennet daughters' position, comfortably brought up but poorly-endowed financially as they are. Claudia Johnson and Susan Wolfson argue, "Mrs Bennet may seem only foolish, vulgar, myopic, and hysteric, but she knows that an unmarried woman is a social abject" (xix). Mrs Bennet seems to grasp only this one economic fact, however, and grossly over-simplifies both her daughters' needs and her own responsibilities as a parent. Moreover, she acts on this solitary perception very ineffectively: certainly she has, at the end of the novel, "'three daughters married!'" (377), but at various points in the novel it looked as if two of those daughters would remain unhappily unmarried and the third end up as a prostitute – largely because of their mother's over-eagerness.

Mr Bennet's flaws as a father are less conventionally treated than those of his wife. His marital unhappiness has apparently left him without the will and energy to fulfil his duties. His one burst of energy, virtually the only exertion he makes as a father in the course of the narrative, apart from his futile journey to London in search of Lydia, is the plea he makes to Elizabeth to marry only when she can do so with respect for her future husband. Apart from this, he seems to have abdicated totally his responsibility as a parent, an abdication made all the easier for him by the fact that his children are daughters, traditionally the responsibility of their mother. He fails in what was accepted as the primary responsibility of a father of the period, that of providing for his children financially: Gisborne speaks of the importance of this duty, quoting St Paul (361–2). He comes to wish that he had "laid by an annual sum, for the better provision of his children, and of his wife, if she survived him" (314) but he has not exerted himself to do so, and his family is inadequately provided for by the marriage settlements. Possibly Mrs Bennet's over-anxiety about marriage might have been allayed by such a measure – but this is to argue beyond the proper bounds of the novel. Mr Bennet also fails ethically in his public displays of contempt for his family.[22] Not only does his behaviour expose his wife to the contempt of her own children but also it exposes both his wife and their children to the contempt of their peers. He refuses to exert himself enough to control or educate either Lydia or Kitty, even when Elizabeth intervenes to beg him to act. As a consequence they both become, as Elizabeth says "'vain, ignorant, idle, and absolutely uncontrouled'" (246). When Lydia seems to be lost forever, he acknowledges as much: "'It has been my own doing, and I ought to feel it'" (307). Elizabeth, perceiving her father's undoubted talents, his wit and intelligence, also perceives "the evils arising from so ill-judged a direction of talents; talents which rightly used, might at least have preserved the respectability of his daughters, even if incapable of enlarging the mind of his wife" (251).[23] Morally Mr Bennet has virtually ceased to be an actor in his personal relationships. He seeks merely passive amusement from other people. When he asks Lizzie rhetorically, "'for what do we live but to make sport for our neighbours, and laugh at them in our turn?'" (364), by the term neighbours he seems unfortunately to include his own family.

Despite the inadequacies of their parents, both Jane and Elizabeth grow to become intelligent, principled and well-mannered young women. Darcy writes to Elizabeth that "to have conducted yourselves so as to avoid any share of the […] censure, is praise no less generally bestowed on you and your eldest sister, than it is honourable to the sense and disposition of both" (218). Austen provides no explicit accounting for the difference between Elizabeth and Jane and their sisters, but it seems feasible enough given their greater intelligence and their family position. Elder children in a large family are often more likely to receive parental care and concern, and to acquire early responsibilities. In any case Elizabeth at least is represented as learning directly from her parents. Through their failures she learns to think about both marriage and parenthood as serious concerns.

***

Virtually nothing in *Sense and Sensibility* is single. Everything appears in a twofold or threefold form.[24] There are two abstract nouns in the title, two heroines, three sets of two sisters, two Mrs Dashwoods, two Elizas, three suitors and so on. So it is appropriate, as well as almost inevitable, that Austen's use of family dysfunction is doubled in this novel, both through the two heroines' encounters with less than perfect families, as in *Northanger Abbey*, and through the heroines' experiences in their own less than perfect family, as in *Pride and*

Prejudice. This double usage of the dysfunctional inevitably involves comparison and contrast, but the contrasts do not present simple oppositions. Few of the many contrasts presented in this novel are either simple or clear-cut.[25] Sense cannot function properly without sensibility and sensibility without sense is a liability. Colonel Brandon, despite his thirty-five-odd years and his flannel waistcoat, is far more romantic than the dashing Willoughby and marries for love, not money. Elinor and Marianne resemble each other greatly in their seriousness,[26] strong feelings and intellectual interests, even though they seem to define themselves not with but against each other, rather as identical twins reared together are said to do. As Rachel Brownstein comments, "each exaggerates and observes and indeed seems deliberately to fashion herself as her sister's opposite" (*Cambridge Companion* 43). So, while in crude terms Elinor's narrative may be described as being shaped by her interaction with the unpleasant Ferrars family, while Marianne's unhappiness comes about rather through her own mother's over-delicate and over-sympathetic refusal to interfere in her relationship with Willoughby, both narratives are far more complex than such an account suggests.

The narratives are further complicated by the slippery nature of the word "family" as it is used in this novel, and especially by the women of the Ferrars family. The four Dashwood women are and are not members of John Dashwood's family. Robert and Edward are and are not their mother's sons. The narrative voice comments sardonically towards the end of the novel that the family of Mrs Ferrars

> had of late been exceedingly fluctuating. For many years of her life she had had two sons; but the crime and annihilation of Edward a few weeks ago, had robbed her of one; the similar annihilation of Robert had left her for a fortnight without any; and now, by the resuscitation of Edward, she had one again. (375)

Mrs Ferrars' daughter, Fanny Dashwood, has an equally flexible view of family and for similar mercenary reasons: her husband's half-sisters, she feels, have no real monetary claim on him at all as "only half blood" (47). On the other hand she feels it unfair that John's "mother" (or stepmother) should have all the household linen and furniture that belonged to their former home. "Family" to such people means those who promote or share one's economic interests.

The Ferrars family has a distorted view of the concept of family, and therefore fails to function as a supportive unit. Both these facts affect Elinor – and the plot – directly. Mrs Ferrars and Fanny Dashwood, though they are both described as physically and intellectually insignificant, are, as Mary

Waldron rightly says, "powerful and dangerous figures" (62). Mrs Ferrars' strongest characteristics are her pride and meanness (254), and two of her children, Robert and Fanny, resemble her. Nature and nurture alike make Fanny Ferrars as selfish and arrogant as her mother. Her husband's half-sisters and their mother leave Sussex for Devon because of the influence of the acquisitive and selfish Fanny on John Dashwood, so that much of the plot of *Sense and Sensibility* is moved on by the unpleasantness of the Ferrars family. Edward Ferrars, the family anomaly, presumably inherits his sense – and his sensibility – from his father, of whom Austen tells us nothing except that he "died very rich" (53). However, Edward unfortunately inherits nothing else, as the family's riches are left entirely in his mother's hands. Mrs Ferrars is quite as controlling a parent in her way as General Tilney is in his. She refuses initially to give either of her sons any financial independence and also refuses to allow Edward "an active profession" (365). His idle state between the ages of 18 and 19, left with "nothing in the world to do, but to fancy [him]self in love," fosters his entanglement with Lucy Steele (365). His financial dependence on a mother who would certainly disapprove of such a connection means that his engagement must be secret. And this secret engagement, which allows him to fall in love with Elinor without allowing him an explanation with her, leads to much of Elinor's suffering in this novel. Elinor's release from this suffering is again brought about in part by the Ferrars family's misbehaviour, a turnabout that indicates the rather sombre nature of this novel's ironic comedy. Mrs Ferrars' excessive anger on discovering Edward's engagement to Lucy leads her to disinherit him, indeed to disown him, and endow her younger and favourite son with £1,000 a year, which encourages Lucy to turn her attention to the conceited Robert. Edward is left free for Elinor.

Elinor's narrative can be read, then, as entirely driven by her encounters with the meanness and stupidity of the Ferrars family. However, the tensions within her immediate family indicated by the novel's title exacerbate her misery. It would be ridiculous to describe the Dashwoods as a dysfunctional family, especially as Austen pointedly contrasts them with the Ferrars (122). Austen represents the mother and her three daughters as living together in a happy, affectionate and equal intellectual companionship, walking, reading, making music and drawing. Edward teases them by saying that an influx of fortune for the Dashwoods would give "'a happy day for booksellers, music-sellers and print-shops'" (123). Isobel Armstrong sees the Dashwood women as being "distinctive – and perhaps not simply distinctive in this text, but among Jane Austen's women figures, in being deliberately presented as thinking, articulate and intellectually aware" (42). It is clear that the two elder daughters' intelligence and discrimination are in part inherited from a mother who certainly fosters these qualities in her daughters. The novel obviously validates these qualities.

All the same, Mrs Dashwood's inability to govern her feelings (44) and her wish to encourage the extremes of feeling in herself and her children mean that Elinor cannot confide in her mother about her unhappiness over Edward's secret engagement. (It would be perfectly possible for her to tell in general terms about her unhappiness without breaking her promise of secrecy to Lucy). Elinor cannot face the added stress that would be caused by the emotionalism and injustice of her family's probable response.

Austen communicates her state of mind with extraordinary accuracy:

> The necessity of concealing from her mother and Marianne, what had been entrusted in confidence to herself, though it obliged her to unceasing exertion, was no aggravation of Elinor's distress. On the contrary it was a relief to her, to be spared the communication of what would give such affliction to them, and to be saved likewise from hearing that condemnation of Edward, which would probably flow from the excess of their partial affection for herself, and which was more than she felt equal to support.
>
> From their counsel, or their conversation she knew she would receive no assistance, their tenderness and sorrow must add to her distress, while her self-command would neither receive encouragement from their example nor from their praise. She was stronger alone. (167)

As Patricia Meyer Spacks argues, "if her divergence from her mother marks Elinor's superiority, it also signals her isolation" (*Boredom* 122). The Dashwoods, the Ferrars family and Lucy Steele have among them pushed Elinor into a position of isolation in which she feels she can neither act nor speak.[27] The outburst, inarticulate as it is, of "tears of joy, which at first she thought would never cease" (363) when she realizes that Edward is free, comes as a relief both to her and to the reader oppressed by an acute sense of Elinor's silence and paralysis. Edward, whose mother's despotism deprives him of financial and professional freedom, and whose engagement deprives him of emotional freedom, is in a similar state of near paralysis, which feeds into his "low spirits" (126).

Marianne, after her discovery of Willoughby's desertion, suffers a parallel state of immobility. Throughout the novel, her feelings tend to take a physical form. In this case it is the pain of physical immobility that she has to endure, required to stay in London when she is longing to go home to Devonshire and her mother, "wildly urgent to be gone" (223). Nevertheless, her mother tells the sisters that they must stay, and this debilitating prolonging of her misery, "the many weeks of previous indisposition which Marianne's disappointment had brought on" (322) that so worry Mrs Jennings, might well be understood as contributing to her serious illness.

This understandable mistake of Mrs Dashwood's is "against the interest of her own individual comfort" (232). Marianne is her favourite daughter. She is, as John Wiltshire writes, "generous and warm-hearted, on good terms with all her daughters, but it is her affinity with Marianne that is continually underlined" *(Body* 26)*:* he describes their relationship as "symbiotic." This close relationship both nourishes and harms Marianne. Her mother sees herself reflected in her beautiful and passionate child, as Mr Bennet sees himself in Elizabeth and Mrs Bennet sees herself in Lydia. A kind of parental narcissism in all these cases leads these parents to foster in their children those elements in which they most resemble themselves.[28] In Elizabeth's case this element is a tendency to look at other people as merely a source of amusement. In Lydia's case it is omnivorous flirting. In the case of Marianne it is of course a matter of sensibility. Mrs Dashwood "value[s] and cherishe[s]" Marianne's excessive sensibility and refuses either to control her own grief at the loss of her husband or to encourage Marianne to control her grief at the loss of her father (44).[29] For Marianne it is natural to suffer intensely, but she learns to suffer excessively from her mother, who has also provided her with a model of narcissistic love that fosters the intensity of her passion for Willoughby, an extension of herself in many ways, with his "natural ardour of mind" (84) and his real or assumed identity of taste with hers. This passion and her excessive suffering over its unhappy ending combine to bring her near death. She comes to understand that

> my own feelings had prepared my sufferings, and that my want of fortitude under them had almost led me to the grave. My illness, I well knew, had been entirely brought on by myself, by such negligence of my own health, as I had felt even at the time to be wrong. Had I died, – it would have been self-destruction. (350)

She comes to blame herself for her "folly," but her mother acknowledges that it was rather her own "imprudence" (355) – imprudence in failing to enquire about Willoughby's history and his possible engagement to Marianne, imprudence in encouraging Marianne's acuteness of feeling – that is to blame.

Marianne's interactions with other families affect her very differently from Elinor. Throughout the novel she is impatient of the ignorance and folly of the various families of her acquaintance, which are indeed patent enough. Sir John Middleton is, as she sees, mindless, Lady Middleton vapid, Mrs Jennings vulgar, Mr Palmer rude, Mrs Palmer silly and so on. But that is not all they are.

Marianne learns painfully that all these defects can coexist with considerable kindness. After her illness, she takes "so particular and lengthened a leave of Mrs Jennings, one so earnestly grateful, so full of respect and kind wishes, as seemed due to her own heart from a secret acknowledgement of past inattention" (346). Later she tells Elinor that her heart had been "'hardened against [the] merits'" of her ordinary acquaintance and her temper "'irritated by their very attention'" (350). As Nancy Struever shows, Marianne's aesthetic sensibilities have blinded her to ordinary human values: "both [Marianne and Mrs Dashwood] err in the overextension of aesthetic competence, which makes Marianne in particular fail in benevolence, Hume's 'most pleasing virtue'" (99). Her interactions with people who are clearly beneath her in terms of intellect and sensitivity, such as the Middletons, Mrs Jennings and Charlotte Palmer, are important in that they eventually make her aware of her misjudgement and imbalanced view of human virtue. Sarah Emsley comments aptly that "*Sense and Sensibility* dramatizes the struggle to love neighbours who are rude, vulgar, senseless and unprincipled, as well as those who are kind, thoughtful, and sensible," in an attempt at Christian charity (59).

In every Austen novel the older generation oppresses the younger to some extent. Any consideration of the complex family dynamics of *Sense and Sensibility* reminds the reader that this novel is especially striking in its presentation of the harm inflicted on the young by their elders. The first Eliza is forced by her uncle and guardian into a marriage with a man she detests. Colonel Brandon's early happiness is destroyed by the same action of his father. Edward spends years of depression and inaction because of his mother, and Elinor and Marianne both endure months of misery partly because of theirs. In *Sense and Sensibility* Austen represents the older generation as robbing the young of the energy and joy to which they are entitled.

Chapter Two

SPOILT CHILDREN: *PRIDE AND PREJUDICE, MANSFIELD PARK* AND *EMMA*

All Jane Austen's novels, to various degrees, explore the problem of the spoilt child – and the spoiling parent – and its effect on family dynamics: consider Isabella Thorpe, Marianne Dashwood, Lydia Bennet, the Bertram sisters, Betsy Price, Elizabeth Elliot and of course Emma Woodhouse. The different kinds of spoiling shown in the various novels are threads in their respective interweavings of significant issues: for instance, Tom Bertram and his sisters are spoiled by the largely materialist values of Mansfield Park (values discussed in Chapter Four), while Elizabeth Elliot is spoiled by the mindless vanity and narcissism of the father she so closely resembles (qualities discussed in Chapter Six).

Austen's treatment of the spoilt child is especially striking in the three novels published in three consecutive years that are the focus of this chapter – *Pride and Prejudice* (1813), *Mansfield Park* (1814) and *Emma* (1815). The interconnection between these three novels is apparent in several ways. In terms of chronology, it seems highly probable that Austen was revising *Pride and Prejudice* during the long period when she was working on *Mansfield Park*, the novel that immediately precedes *Emma*.[1] In this series of novels, Jane Austen responds, as was indeed her habit, to each previous achievement not by producing more of the same, but by providing counter-models, which work as antidotes to any over-simplistic understanding of the characters and situations she has already explored in earlier novels. She is, as Claudia Johnson writes, "a profoundly experimental novelist" ("What Became" 63). Looking at these three novels as a sequence, we see her conceiving ideas and interactions, developing them and qualifying them. Each novel in itself presents a multi-faceted view of human character and relationships. Read together, they provide an even more complex view of social interactions. As an obvious example, after her brilliant and deservedly successful portrayal of the vivacious and energetic Elizabeth Bennet in *Pride and Prejudice*,[2] Austen's next novel implies that Elizabeth's vitality is essential neither to successful fiction nor to the moral life, for in *Mansfield Park* she creates in Fanny Price a heroine who, for all her intelligence and intensity, is shy, quiet and sickly – and who could never be accused, as

Elizabeth is twice, of anything like wildness. Meanwhile Austen bestows Elizabeth's overflowing health and lively wit on the anti-heroine, the worldly Mary Crawford. As Lionel Trilling said long ago, "to outward seeming, Mary Crawford of *Mansfield Park* is another version of Elizabeth Bennet" (213), but of course the emphasis here must be on the "outward seeming."[3] When in her subsequent novel Austen creates another vigorous and outspoken heroine like Elizabeth, she immediately ensures that no one will share Emma's views of her own perfection: as Marilyn Butler says, "with Emma there is no danger, as there is with Elizabeth, that the reader will fail to see the heroine's mistakes for what they are" (250).

The series of father figures in these three novels, a concern that will be developed at length in the three chapters of Part II, is also instructive. The ironical and lax Mr Bennet is followed by the humourless and authoritarian Sir Thomas Bertram. In each case the very different paternal inadequacies – inadequacies both these fathers are eventually forced to recognize – are represented as inadvertently fostering sexual misadventures in their daughters. However, in the third novel, Mr Woodhouse manages to restrict his daughter's activities more effectively than either Mr Bennet or Sir Thomas through exercising the power of feebleness of mind, body and spirit.

The interconnection between these three novels is especially significant in considering another series of transformations involving the issue of the spoilt child, the central concern of this chapter. The fallen woman of *Mansfield Park* passes on many of her qualities and conditions of life to the heroine of *Emma*, while in developing the characters of both Maria Bertram and Emma Woodhouse, Austen works out more fully ideas she first explores in *Pride and Prejudice*, ideas concerning what might be called the disadvantages of the advantaged. Her treatment of these spoilt children – Darcy, Maria, Emma – has retained the power to disturb her comfortable and privileged readers through two centuries.[4]

* * *

Towards the end of *Pride and Prejudice*, after Elizabeth has accepted his second proposal of marriage, Mr Darcy shows how completely her angry rejection of his first proposal has shattered his complacency, driving him towards self-examination and greater self-knowledge. Like the novel as a whole – like all Austen's novels – this love scene focuses not so much on manifestations of lovers' behaviour as on an account of love as a process of moral transformation. Austen represents Darcy as responding to the shock of Elizabeth's attack on his "ungentlemanly behaviour" by attempting to discover for himself the seeds of his adult weaknesses and finding them in his upbringing and childhood experiences. Clearly Darcy sees himself as having been reared and educated with love and care, brought up as he is as the only son of doting parents amid the comfort and beauty of Pemberley, in the comfortable knowledge that he is the heir to this beloved home. Yet Austen carefully shows him as coming to the belief that all the same, despite this love and care, he has never needed or been encouraged to question himself or his self-importance. He comes to acknowledge the drawbacks of such an unexamined life, as he gradually perceives his habitual insensitivity to the feelings of most other people – his failure in attention to them, that is.[5] In the first delight of accepted love he says to Elizabeth:

> I have been a selfish being all my life, in practice, though not in principle. As a child I was taught what was *right*, but I was not taught to correct my temper. I was given good principles, but left to follow them in pride and conceit. Unfortunately an only son (for many years an only *child*) I was spoilt by my parents, who though good themselves [...] allowed, encouraged, almost taught me to be selfish and overbearing, to care for none beyond my own family circle, to think meanly of all the rest of the world, to *wish* at least to think meanly of their sense and worth compared with my own. Such I was from eight to eight and twenty; and such I might still have been but for you, dearest, loveliest Elizabeth. What do I not owe you! (368 – Austen's emphases)

Christopher Ricks regards this confession as coexisting uneasily with the comments of the housekeeper at Pemberley, Mrs Reynolds, who says she has "never had a cross word from him" (101–2). It is unlikely, however, that the average reader has any problem in making these two accounts jibe. Courtesy to servants and consideration towards dependents, people who are, after all, to some extent within his "own family circle," are not incompatible with a sense of superiority towards the outside world. The selfishness Darcy admits to is not precisely solipsistic: it is selfishness only if the "self" in question includes his own family, a point I will develop later. The change of attitude he claims to have undergone as a result of his relations with Elizabeth involves a greater consideration for "all the rest of the world." It is as important for him morally as it is for Elizabeth materially and emotionally that their marriage is exogamous, taking them both well beyond their accustomed family circles.

Darcy's analysis of the effects of his upbringing is strikingly similar in many respects to a crucial passage in *Mansfield Park*, a novel that is generally acknowledged as being directly concerned with the popular contemporary theme of education, far more so than is *Pride and Prejudice*.[6] Most of Kenneth Moler's lengthy discussion of *Mansfield Park* is devoted to the theme of education

(*Art of Allusion* 109–54), for instance, while Marilyn Butler begins her treatment of the novel by pointing out that to a contemporary of Austen's it might well be seen as "yet another novel by a female about female education" (219). Peter Knox-Shaw broadens the discussion of *Mansfield Park* and education and links it not with the fiction of Austen's female contemporaries, but rather with the eighteenth-century sceptical tradition: "There is no novel written before *Mansfield Park* (and few after it) which can begin to match its account of the power of nurture – a concept central to the Anglo-Scottish school" (Knox-Shaw 189). The neglect and unkindness doled out to the ten-year-old Fanny, the flattery and overindulgence of Maria and Julia as children, prepare them – and the reader – for their adult selves. In a novel such as this, in which education in its broadest sense is central, a parent's view of his own performance is especially illuminating. In Sir Thomas Bertram's analysis of his daughters' upbringing, following Maria's adultery and Julia's elopement, he faces his own faults and deficiencies as a parent. He first realizes the evil of the contrast between his own severity towards his children and Mrs Norris's leniency, which has led to the children's loss of confidence in him. Sir Thomas's – or Austen's – insight echoes Mary Wollstonecraft's comment that "unless a mother concur, the father who restrains will ever be considered a tyrant" (339). (In the case of Maria and Julia it is a mother-figure who fails to "concur.") Sir Thomas goes on, however, to reflect that

> bad as it was [...] it had not been the most direful mistake in his plan of education. Something must have been wanting *within*, or time would have worn away much of its ill effect. He feared that principle, active principle, had been wanting, that they had never been properly taught to govern their inclinations and tempers, by that sense of duty which can alone suffice. They had been instructed theoretically in their religion, but never required to bring it into daily practice. To be distinguished for elegance and accomplishments – the authorized object of their youth – could have no useful influence that way, no moral effect on the mind. He had meant them to be good, but his cares had been directed to the understanding and manners, not the disposition; and of the necessity of self-denial and humility, he feared they had never heard from any lips that could profit them. (459)

The moral terms ascribed to Sir Thomas in this passage are commonplace enough in a period still strongly influenced by Locke's writings on education.[7] Wollstonecraft, for instance, argues that "the temper, in particular, requires the most judicious attention" (290). Thomas Gisborne, writing in 1797 about the duties of a mother rather than a father, suggests that an important aspect of parental duties is "the regulation of the daughter's disposition and the improvement of her heart" (*Enquiry* 370). Hannah More deplores the neglect of "the dispositions of the mind," which means that "indications of the temper are not properly cherished nor the affections of the heart sufficiently regulated" (*Letters to Young Ladies* 78). Austen actualizes such generalizations, draining them of their facile quality, by showing a parent with principle and intellect enough to accept the necessity of these duties but without moral stamina or insight enough to act on them. His self-analysis shows Sir Thomas in the painful process of realizing in the last chapter of the novel a fact Austen has made plain to the reader much earlier, both through action and through narrative comment: "It is not very wonderful," says the narrative voice, commenting on Fanny Price's early days at Mansfield, "that with all their promising talents and early information, they [Julia and Maria] should be entirely deficient in the less common acquirements of self-knowledge, generosity and humility" (50). By this point, their conceit and complacency have become quite evident in any case by their treatment of their lonely little cousin and their easy assumption of total superiority over her.

Sir Thomas Bertram's belated analysis of his faults as a parent is remarkably close to Darcy's consideration of his own childhood, considering the striking difference of the young people involved. Both analyses stress the harm done to a moral education by dependence on theory rather than practice; both stress the inadequate grounding in controlling the temper; both stress "the necessity of [...] humility." The emphasis in Mr Darcy's self-analysis is naturally on the pride and exclusiveness that he has found so damaging in his relationship with Elizabeth, whom he is addressing. Sir Thomas, on the other hand, is more concerned with the false sense of values and uncontrolled inclinations fostered in his daughters, whose selfishness is more literally *self*ish than Darcy's exclusiveness. Despite inevitable differences, both passages communicate a sense of the profound importance of acquiring and acting upon humility, and suggest the difficulty with which any sense of humility – which is to say a sense of one's own minor role in the great scheme of things – can be instilled in children as well-endowed by both nature and circumstance as are the Bertram children and Darcy.[8]

Such privileged children are likely to retain well into adulthood the egotism of infancy, which prevents them from perceiving the reality of other people. Tom Bertram does eventually learn to think, but not until the age of twenty-six. This transformation comes about only through suffering a serious illness and through his distress at Maria's catastrophe. And, of course, in *Mansfield Park*, William, Fanny and Susan Price are present to demonstrate to Sir Thomas "the advantages of early hardship and discipline, and the consciousness of being born to struggle and to endure" (456). In a novel in which, as John Wiltshire reminds us, nearly all the characters are very rich (*Cambridge Companion* 59), only those who lack wealth lack its disadvantages.[9] The solitary exception is Edmund Bertram, whose comparative unselfishness seems to be the result of a combination of his inferior position as second son and his sense of his vocation as a clergyman. Sir Thomas's thoughts about the benefits of hardship certainly accord with a narrative in which the poorest, weakest, least pretty, least well-born girl is its heroine.

Austen goes on to explore a totally different case in *Emma*, in which the heroine is, superficially at least, far closer to Maria than to Fanny. Indeed, Maria Bertram and Emma Woodhouse are strikingly alike in many ways. Both young women, through their social standing and their dominating natures, are leaders in their own small worlds: "no one loved better to lead than Maria" (*MP* 161), while "in every respect it suited Emma best to lead" (*E* 218). They are also the prettiest young women in their own regular circle: the Miss Bertrams are "the finest young women in the country" (72) and, of the two sisters, Maria is "certainly the handsomest," according to Mr Crawford, something of a connoisseur in these matters (73). The Bertram sisters and Emma are the richest young women around in their separate rural spheres. Maria and Emma are also considerably brighter than many of their daily companions, though in both cases their intelligence is clouded by their comfortable complacency. In the case of Maria Bertram, the narrative voice informs us of her cleverness – her "promising talents and early information" (50), while Mr Knightley and Mrs Weston, her most intelligent companions, both acknowledge Emma's ability. In any case, Austen shows Emma's cleverness in her occasionally cruel wit as well as her lively if unfounded inventions. Indeed, it is her intelligence, rather than her fortune or her beauty, that Mr Knightley blames, when talking to Mrs Weston, for spoiling her:

> Emma is spoiled by being the cleverest of her family. At ten years old, she had the misfortune of being able to answer questions which puzzled her sister at seventeen. She was always quick and assured: Isabella slow and diffident. And ever since she was twelve, Emma has been mistress of the house and of you all. In her mother she lost the only person able to cope with her. She inherits her mother's talents, and must have been under subjection to her. (80)

We may resist as over-moralistic Mr Knightley's idea of Emma's intellect being a misfortune, but Austen insists that her readers at least engage with this assessment.[10] There is some degree of justice behind Knightley's angry retort to Emma: "'Better be without sense, than misapply it as you do'" (99). Mr Knightley sees that Emma's understanding of other people's behaviour and motives is warped not only by her position as the most talented member of her family and the richest young woman in the neighbourhood, but by the special treatment that is the result of her good looks. She is "a pretty young woman" and therefore more especially "a spoiled child" (126); as such she is likely to be slow in perceiving the truth of situations.

All of Maria's and Emma's privileged "disadvantages" have already appeared in Austen's representation of Darcy. He is explicitly more handsome and more clever than his nearest peer in the novel, Mr Bingley. He is also more than twice as rich.[11] In fact, in three consecutive novels Jane Austen chooses to deal with young people who have apparently all the social, physical and intellectual advantages to a high degree and who are, to a varying extent, spoilt by the excessive self-esteem and related blindness to other people arising from these very advantages. *Emma* famously begins with an outspoken indication of these advantages – "Emma Woodhouse, handsome, clever, and rich, with a comfortable home and happy disposition seemed to unite some of the best blessings of existence" (53). This beginning is followed by a pretty clear indication of the intrinsic drawbacks of these blessings: "the power of having rather too much her own way, and a disposition to think a little too well of herself; these were the disadvantages which threatened alloy to her many enjoyments" (55). Once again, Emma's conceit threatens her own happiness as well as her moral development. In *Emma*, the flawed perceptions of the spoilt child who gives the novel its name provide its entire plot. *Emma* works out fully the theme of the disadvantages of privilege which Austen had begun to explore in *Pride and Prejudice* through Darcy and in *Mansfield Park* through the Bertram girls, who certainly have "rather too much of their own way."

* * *

And yet for all their similarities, we cannot for one moment imagine Emma meeting with poor Maria's eventual fate. Maria's narrative is conventional: she is rich and pretty, succumbs to the temptations associated with rich and pretty young women in eighteenth-century novels, materialism and vanity, and is punished as they are.[12] Emma's narrative is far more original: she is neither vain nor especially materialistic, and her errors are largely the result of her combination of intelligence and inexperience.[13] Maria's is a tragic narrative, although notoriously the tragedy is pushed ruthlessly and explicitly into the margins of the novel in which it is enacted: "Let other pens dwell on guilt and misery" (457). Emma's is essentially a comic narrative. Like Mr Darcy, Emma eventually overcomes her disadvantages as a spoilt child and like him she achieves this largely through her relationship with her future spouse. Sexual love and the fear of losing the beloved eventually force them both into applying their intelligence to their own motives and behaviour and "the resolution of [their] own better conduct" (*Emma* 361). Through self-examination they both acquire a degree of self-knowledge and humility. Maria Bertram never comes to such self-examination or such resolution – tellingly it is her father who will reflect on her development, not she herself. And for Maria Bertram – Maria Rushworth as she so unfortunately becomes – sexual love is catastrophic, ruinous. The passionate nature that she had so carefully and successfully hidden from her father is not related to the rest of her life, and therefore it becomes destructive. It is the nature rather than the degree of Maria's love that is destructive, and, as with Austen's other characters, the nature of her sexual love is directly related to the nature of her other loves.

Except now the question is, what other loves? For Maria shows no real affection for any other character in the novel. For Austen, loving sibling relations are something of a touchstone of character, and while Maria and Julia are usually "on easy terms" (181), the weakness of the bond between them becomes apparent through their rivalry over Mr Crawford. For both of them, sexual love comes first, and neither of them has "affection or principle enough to make them merciful or just, to give them honour or compassion" in this triangular game (181). Maria shows no more affection for her brothers; she enjoys, like Tom, the triumph of witnessing the overthrow of Edmund's scruples over *Lovers' Vows* by his jealousy over Miss Crawford, which robs him of his "moral elevation" (177). More seriously, neither sister shows enough concern over Tom's potentially fatal illness to leave their pleasures in London and visit him, as Mary Crawford, a genuinely affectionate sister, observes (433). They show no affection for the aunt who indulges and flatters them – though indeed Mrs Norris's tragedy seems to be that she can never inspire affection. No more do they care for their mother, for that matter, while the narrative voice explicitly states that "their father was no object of love to them, he had never seemed the friend of their pleasures, and his absence was unhappily most welcome" (61). Maria's loveless marriage is unsurprising, given her lack of ordinary family affection and the mores of her society. Perhaps it is because of this essential coldness in Maria that many readers, while understanding entirely her longing for independence and liberty, find it hard to sympathize with her entirely. This deficiency in ordinary family feeling is shown more sharply in the light of the Crawfords' strong if unscrupulous affection for each other and the sisterly love of Mrs Grant for them both. It contrasts even more strongly with the devoted and happy fraternal love between Fanny and William Price, and the growing attachment between Fanny and Susan.

Maria Bertram has never received much real affection and for this very reason she has not much affection to give. No child would mistake the flattery of Mrs Norris, who "never knew how to be pleasant to children" (56), or Lady

Bertram's indolence, or even Sir Thomas's conscientious but chilly care, for normal spontaneous parental love. So while Darcy and Emma are spoilt by material privileges combined with parental doting Maria is spoilt by material privileges combined with parental coldness. Initially the result of this early chill is merely that she and Julia "had no idea of carrying their obliging manners to the sacrifice of any real pleasure" (64): their manners have no relations to morals. But eventually, in combination with her "strong passions" – her sexual feelings – this incapacity for warmth leads to her destructive love for Henry Crawford, a love that is all passion and no affection. Maria shows no more concern for Henry Crawford's happiness than she does for her husband's – or than either of them does for hers. She is certainly aware that her liaison with Crawford is destructive to both of them, and even comes to take a vindictive pleasure in the fact that it ruins her lover's chances of real happiness with Fanny (459–60).

The nature of Emma's affections is more complex. To some critics she has seemed cold, and certainly Austen establishes through her relationships with many other characters Emma's basic indifference to their feelings and their natures – her failure in attention to their situations. She is often more interested in her own amusing fantasies than in the humdrum reality of Highbury, at least as far as Mr Elton, Frank Churchill, Harriet Smith, Jane Fairfax and the Bateses are concerned. Towards most of the inhabitants of Highbury she is indeed cold for much of the novel; she finds it hard to be kind to the Bateses because she sees her obligations to them entirely as a matter of duty and not of affection or compassion (one may compare her real compassion for the working poor). Towards the world in general, the world outside her own family, like Darcy, Emma is blind as well as cold, until she is compelled to break through her spoilt child's complacency and examine her assumptions and her behaviour.

Yet from the very first scene of the novel onwards, Austen represents Emma as a person capable of great warmth and exceptionally intelligent and generous affection. Her love of home is, as Julia Prewitt Brown argues, "just as strong as her love of self" (*Approaches* 22). Through Emma's combination of loving thoughtfulness, wit and wilfulness, Austen compels our interest in her from the first chapter onwards, preventing us from finding her interfering and conceited ways totally repellent. Her first appearance establishes that she is a most affectionate and considerate daughter. She expresses her love with intelligent care and energy, exerting herself to keep her father cheerful and, as far as possible, rational. She is an affectionate friend to Miss Taylor and a loving sister and aunt. Mr Knightley, seeing her with a baby niece (a little Emma), comments, "'if you were as much guided by nature in your estimate of men and women, and as little under the power of fancy and whim in your dealings with them, as you are where these children are concerned, we might always think alike'" (126), meaning that Emma might think correctly. In the maturity of her love, Emma acknowledges Knightley's role in her upbringing: "'I had the assistance of all your endeavours to counteract the indulgence of other people'" (389). Knightley, however, believes that his interference "'was quite as likely to do harm as good'" (389).

James Boyd White argues, "Emma shows at the beginning that she can recognize and respond to the circumstances of another when she treats her father as she does, and she exhibits similar qualities both in visiting the family stricken by illness and poverty and in the way she talks about them. But she lacks this sort of kindness in her other relations, in part because true kindness requires observation and a true understanding of one's own condition" (190). Emma sees her father and the poor family clearly because she is driven to look closely at them, paying proper attention to her father because of proximity and affection and to the poor because of their obvious needs. Emma's dealings with other middle-class people outside her family are "under the power of fancy and whim" because she sees them not as persons deserving attention, but as clay that she can model, or as actors in the drama she wishes to see performed. She sees them with the artist's eye though she lacks the artist's necessary self-discipline. She relates to other people instrumentally, not as ends in themselves but as possible sources of amusement, like Mr Bennet, another abuser of his own intelligence: "'For what do we live, but to make sport for our neighbours and to laugh at them in our turn?'" (*P&P* 364). Because Emma's neighbours are so humdrum, such poor material, she has to manipulate them in an attempt to make them oblige. She is "guided by nature" – by attention to the realities of a situation – only when she is guided by love – that is, in her treatment of her family, Mrs Weston and Mr Knightley. By the end of the novel she is beginning to acquire enough humility to see human beings in general as persons to be respected. She achieves maturity when she can extend the recognition of other people as persons beyond her own little circle. Austen stresses through Emma's development, as she had earlier done through Mr Darcy's, the immaturity of exclusiveness, the maturity of inclusiveness.[14]

***

Emma is able to mature in this way because she has a basis; she has a circle to extend. Unlike Maria Bertram, whose circle of love encloses only herself, from her earliest days Emma has received and given love, that is, she has necessarily accepted some other people as persons. Because she has learnt at the proper early age to recognize other selves, once her shell of complacency and self-satisfied exclusiveness is broken down through a more potent love, she is able to see beyond her own circle. She eventually acknowledges Frank Churchill and Jane Fairfax, Harriet Smith and Robert Martin for what they are.

This same initial tendency "to care for none beyond [one's] own family circle, to think meanly of all the rest of the world," is something Emma shares with Mr Darcy, whose words these are (*P&P* 368). The narrative voice informs us early on that Darcy is "haughty, reserved, and fastidious," and that "his manners, though well bred, were not inviting" (55). This exclusiveness is overcome, as he acknowledges, by one whom his fastidiousness might well have led him to reject entirely – and indeed does lead him to reject initially – his "'dearest, loveliest Elizabeth.'" But his love for Elizabeth is not the only love of his life, any more than Emma's love for Mr Knightley is the only love of hers. He has been a beloved and loving son and is a very affectionate brother. He speaks "with affectionate praise of his sister's proficiency" (197) as a musician, and delights in refurnishing a sitting-room for her. The housekeeper at Pemberley says: "'Whatever can give his sister any pleasure, is sure to be done in a moment. There is nothing he would not do for her'" (263). He is also a real friend to Mr Bingley, and if his friendship also has some of the patronizing quality of his relationship with his much younger sister, then this is partly the almost inevitable result of his social and intellectual superiority over his friend. Like Emma, he starts out with a diminished capacity for respecting other people, but this capacity grows through the course of the novel; and again it is able to grow because it has some soil in which to grow.

The domestic circle is naturally the most likely place for such a nature to reveal itself in the most flattering, and also perhaps the clearest light. For this reason it is at Pemberley that Elizabeth Bennet first sees Darcy as a possible object of love: her teasing remark to Jane, that her onset of love dates from first "'seeing his beautiful grounds at Pemberley'" (372), is quite clearly a playful version of the truth. Only at Pemberley can both the barriers indicated by the novel's title finally be surmounted. At Pemberley, Elizabeth's perceptions are no longer distorted by prejudice, but, more importantly, the object of her perceptions has changed, partly because of his wish to please her, but also because in his own home circle Mr Darcy's behaviour is no longer distorted by the pride and disdain of all beyond the family circle, which made his manners and assumptions at Meryton, Netherfield, Hunsford Parsonage and even occasionally at Rosings, hurtful and inappropriate. At Pemberley he is revealed as no longer reserved and suspicious but as affectionate, thoughtful, good-tempered and charitable, because he is at home and has a proper and habitual arena for exercising these qualities. Away from home he perceives the faults and vulgarities of others, but at home he perceives the needs of others and can usually fulfil them; like Emma at Hartfield, he is a considerate host. Elizabeth loves Darcy only when she sees his full reality: and the full reality of such spoilt children is very much restricted in the early stages of their lives. Maria Bertram is unlike the other two spoilt children considered here in that her perception of reality is not enhanced or notably changed by her home or her family – on the contrary. Unlike Darcy and Emma she dislikes her home and longs to escape from it – and for good reason: Mansfield Park is cold and restrictive. This detachment from her family is part of the disastrous preparation for her disastrous marriage: "in all the important preparations of the mind she was complete; being prepared for matrimony by an hatred of home, restraint, and tranquility; by the misery of disappointed affection, and contempt of the man she was to marry" (218).

In brief, Mr Darcy, like Emma, has never been quite shut in on himself. He has been loved and he has loved, and can therefore grow in his capacity for love. Whereas poor Maria, who, though indulged and flattered, has been deprived of genuine affection, ends up with a quite infernal punishment, incarcerated with the person who is largely responsible for her damagingly exaggerated sense of her own powers and importance:

> It ended in Mrs Norris's resolving to quit Mansfield, and devote herself to her unfortunate Maria, and in an establishment being formed with them in another country – remote and private, where, shut up together with little society, on one side no affection, on the other no judgement, it may be reasonably supposed that their tempers became their mutual punishment. (261)

From them that have not shall be taken away even that which they have.[15]

* * *

The situation and development of Mr Darcy evidently continued to fascinate his creator. Through it she could question a particular aspect of family and social dynamics. She could also scrutinize the ordinary operating system of values and undermine the easy assumption that it is necessarily in all ways best to be the prettiest or most handsome, the richest, the most clever or to have the strongest will. And so she continues to work out more fully what happens to the spoilt child in her two subsequent novels. Like Darcy, Maria and Emma have all these advantages, and like him they suffer for them. In the central narratives of the novels in which they appear, Maria Bertram is certainly a less important character than Mr Darcy, but Austen explores the nature and the results of her upbringing in far greater detail, while the results, both good and bad, of Emma's spoiling is the very centre of the novel that bears her name.

All three characters share a common failing of the young and clever: because they are more able than many of their companions, they find it easy to overestimate their own superiority and undervalue other people. Emma and Mr Darcy are rescued from this narrow perspective, this incapacity to recognize other people as feeling persons, by a love that forces them eventually to apply their considerable intelligence to their own characters and see their own deficiencies. This kind of intelligent love is possible for them because they have some practice in loving, because they have themselves been loved. Austen's implication in such narratives is that what matters is not so much being prettiest, cleverest or richest as being the most loving. And this aspect of her theme is continued in the character of Anne Elliot in *Persuasion*, the only member of her family to care for anything beyond herself and indeed to see anything beyond herself.

"In essence the *action* of all six of Jane Austen's novels is the same," says Marilyn Butler (166; emphasis in the original); that is, according to Butler, each novel works towards one character (or more) discovering his or her delusions. The delusions of Catherine Morland in *Northanger Abbey* and Marianne Dashwood in *Sense and Sensibility* are produced by a combination of their extreme youth, their failure to question their reading and their respective family situations. In *Persuasion*, Wentworth's delusions come from a combination of his long-lasting anger with Anne and his refusal to question his own judgment or change his mind. In the three novels under discussion, through the characters and narratives of Mr Darcy, Maria and Emma, Austen examines not just a particular kind of delusion at work but also its roots in early childhood. Like the work of other imaginative writers of her lifetime, major and minor – writers such as Wordsworth, Coleridge, Wollstonecraft, Mary Shelley and Maria Edgeworth – Austen's novels are a significant part of a contemporary discourse on child development, including both formal education and parental participation and its effects on both character and destiny. Austen, in the three completed novels of her maturity, shows how people survive, or fail to survive, one of the more subtle and persistent forms of parental abuse.

Chapter Three

"USEFULNESS AND EXERTION": MOTHERS AND SISTERS IN *SENSE AND SENSIBILITY*, *MANSFIELD PARK*, *EMMA* AND *PERSUASION*

Early in her career, Jane Austen created in *Lady Susan* one of the worst and most entertaining of fictional mothers.[1] Among Austen's critics, indeed, there is a tendency to regard the mothers in all her novels as being either bad or dead.[2] "Competent mothering is something of a death sentence for a woman" in Austen's novels, according to Peter Graham (67), alluding to the deaths of Lady Elliot, Mrs Woodhouse and Mrs Tilney.[3] Jan Fergus reads Austen's tendency to subtract the mother either through death or through absence as a narrative device in the tradition of the eighteenth-century novel of self-education, noting that the presence of an effective mother "would prevent the heroine from error and thus from educating herself" (89).[4] This comment certainly applies to *Northanger Abbey*, for Catherine must be taken from her large and happy family and her excellent mother before she can learn a little about life and begin to grow up.

Austen's other novels, however, diverge from the eighteenth-century tradition that Fergus discusses. In these more complex explorations of family life the mothers of the heroines, whether present or absent, influence their daughters' narratives powerfully. In virtually any family, the presence or absence, as well as the character, of the mother affects the children both as individuals and in relation to each other. In the four novels discussed here Austen represents the mother as a determining factor in the relations between her daughters. Moreover, in these novels the mother affects her daughter's sense of domestic obligations, whether directly or indirectly. It is through the figure of the mother and her attitude to her familial obligations that the protagonists acquire the sense of their traditional domestic obligations – the "usefulness and exertion" of this chapter's title.

Usefulness and exertion are important principles implicit throughout Austen's novels, as applied to both the practical and the moral life. Stuart Tave writes that, in Austen's fiction, "the moral life is a purposeful and powerful pursuit, a life of activity, of usefulness, of exertion" (98).[5] Austen repeatedly emphasizes the moral value of practical exertion by contrasting it with self-indulgence. Henry Crawford, for instance, compares ruefully his own selfish love of pleasure with the "usefulness" and "exertion" of young William Price (*MP* 249); the idle extravagance of Sir Walter Elliot contrasts with the active service of the naval officers; the hard-working Robert Martin and Mr Knightley command more respect than the frivolous Frank Churchill.

Usefulness and exertion are essential values for women as well as for men. Men's responsibilities are usually comparatively clear. The obligations of landowners such as Mr Darcy, Sir Thomas Bertram, and Mr Knightley, sailors such as Captain Wentworth and William Price, or clergymen such as Edmund Bertram and Edward Ferrars are generally recognized. For the women of this class, the gentry and pseudo-gentry of whom Austen writes,[6] their practical and social responsibilities were on the whole more uniform, differing only in accordance with the family's income and the talents and energy of the women themselves.[7] Such women, if they married, would become the mistress of the house with the consequent social, economic and domestic responsibilities: for running a comfortable household, for social arrangements, including social status and social contacts,[8] for the household's financial probity,[9] for the moral and social training and general education of the children. Writers of all shades of belief considered the latter the most important female obligation: "one of the grand duties annexed to the female character by nature," according to Mary Wollstonecraft (290) and "the great object [...] to which you [women] are called," according to Hannah More (*Strictures* 1.52).[10] With the marriages that end these novels – and sometimes before – the heroines embark on a life of such responsibilities. The mother in such a household would necessarily influence her daughters' ideas of their domestic role and responsibilities, through precept and through example, either positive or negative, and in Austen's novels she influences them in life and in death.

The death of the mother drastically changes the family dynamics, giving a measure of power and freedom and the capacity for practical usefulness to the eldest unmarried daughter, a phenomenon to be examined in relation both to *Persuasion* and to *Emma*. In the other two novels discussed here the mother is alive, but there is a similar disruption in predictable family dynamics affecting a daughter's sense of herself and her personal value. In *Mansfield Park*, the heroine is separated from her mother for much of the narrative. In *Sense and Sensibility*, Mrs Dashwood's character and her newly widowed state place a burden of practical and moral usefulness on Elinor, which changes the dynamics of the Dashwood family. The position of the mother profoundly affects the sense of usefulness and the effective exertions of Anne, Emma, Fanny and Elinor as well as their interactions with their sisters.

* * *

The death or absence of the mother is more than an emotional loss. It involves an upheaval in the whole structure of the family. In *Persuasion* and *Emma*, the two novels centred on motherless daughters, Austen establishes this important fact about the heroine's life immediately. In *Emma* it is mentioned briefly in explanation of Emma's position. In *Persuasion*, however, which is a novel of extended mourning and renewed hope, the dead mother is a more important figure. The novel begins with the living father – and the baronetage – but then moves at once to Lady Elliot, suggesting immediately the mother's role, her character and the implications of her death:

> Lady Elliot had been an excellent woman, sensible and amiable, whose judgment and conduct, if they might be pardoned the youthful infatuation that made her Lady Elliot, had never required indulgence afterwards. – She had humoured, or softened, or concealed his failings, and promoted his real respectability for seventeen years; and, though not the very happiest being herself, had found enough in her duties, her friends, and her children, to attach her to life, and to make it no matter of indifference to her when she was called upon to quit them. – Three girls, the eldest sixteen and fourteen, was an awful legacy for a mother to bequeath; an awful charge rather, to confide to the authority and guidance of a conceited, silly father. (47)

Austen establishes the duty of the female head of such a household as Kellynch Hall both to provide her husband, through such social and economic power as she has, with a dignity that he might not possess in himself, and to guide her growing children. With Lady Elliot's death Sir Walter loses much of his "real respectability" to his own idleness and extravagance, and both her eldest and youngest daughters are left unchecked in their separate versions of the "Elliot pride" (118).

Anne, the middle daughter, suffers differently. She grieves intensely for the mother she resembles. Her dislike of Bath arises in part from her memories of being sent there to school when she was "grieving for a mother whom she had dearly loved [...] suffering as a girl of fourteen, of strong sensibility and not high spirits, must suffer at such a time" (173). Her fast-fading spark of pleasure at the thought of marrying Mr Elliot arises from love of her mother and her home rather than any minimal attraction to her cousin:

> The idea of becoming what her mother had been; of having the precious name of "Lady Elliot" first revived in herself; of being restored to Kellynch, calling it her home again, her home for ever, was a charm which she could not immediately resist [...] The [...] image of Mr Elliot

speaking for himself brought Anne to composure again. The charm of Kellynch and of "Lady Elliot" all faded away. She never could accept him. (180)

Yet the death of Lady Elliot represents more than a personal loss for Anne. It has also changed her place in the family, severely restricted her capacity for effective activity and left her in a position of impotence. All the mother's power devolves according to convention on her eldest daughter so that Elizabeth at sixteen has become the mistress of Kellynch Hall, "presiding and directing with a self-possession and decision [...] laying down the domestic law at home" (49). Elizabeth's narcissism, a reflection of her father's, means that she lacks respect for sisters who do not resemble her and whom she regards as inferior in the only two concerns that matter to her, social position and personal appearance. Her "domestic law" excludes Anne from power as well as from any pleasure their position might offer, such as the annual visit to London. Elizabeth's traditional position of authority as mistress of the house is strongly reinforced by her father's preference for her: "being very handsome and very like himself her influence was great" (48), while Anne "was nobody with either father or sister: her word had no weight; her convenience was always to give way; –she was only Anne" (48).

This treatment robs Anne of affection; she is drawn to Captain Wentworth partly because "she had hardly any body to love" (65). It also robs her of power and usefulness, as she is allowed no proper role in the functioning of the household. She has no control over the family expenditures and cannot curtail the extravagances that push the Elliots headlong into debt. After their money matters reach a crisis, she is consulted neither about the necessary economies nor about the choice of residence and arrangements for the move: "Nobody will want her in Bath," according to Elizabeth (72). In a novel in which Austen gently emphasizes the value of useful activity through the repeated contrast between the idleness and "heartless elegance" of the elder Elliots and the industry and utility of the naval officers, Anne's marginal position becomes especially significant.

Anne's virtual impotence is particularly frustrating because she has exceptional capacities that she can rarely exercise. Unlike either of her sisters, she inherits Lady Elliot's intelligence and practical ability. She has also learnt a sense of financial morality from her mother, who had arranged matters so that in her lifetime "there had been method, moderation, and economy, which had just kept [Sir Walter] within his income" (51). It is Anne who, caring only for "justice and equity" to their creditors (53), tries to insist on rigid economies when she is finally informed of the extent of the family debts. Meanwhile those who have incurred the debts, Sir Walter and Elizabeth, feel "ill-used and unfortunate" and refuse to consider any changes that affect either their comfort or their idea of their own dignity (52).

Anne's desire and ability to care for people seems to have been inherited or learned from the mother who was so concerned about the guidance of her children. Although Anne has no acknowledged use or function in her daily life within her family, Austen repeatedly represents her as engaged in useful activity. In various ways and to various degrees, she looks after her sister Mary, her little nephew Charles, Louisa and Henrietta Musgrove, the Musgrove parents, Captain Benwick and Mrs Smith. Before she leaves Kellynch, she is busy copying a catalogue of books and pictures, giving the gardener instructions, sorting books and music, re-packing and lastly "going to almost every house in the parish as a sort of take-leave" (76). This final comment shows that Anne's sense of responsibility goes beyond the immediate domestic environment to the wider community. While most of the pleasure of the ending of *Persuasion* comes from the long delayed fulfilment of the love between Anne and Captain Wentworth, some comes from her release from a family in which, ever since her mother's death, her social, emotional, domestic and practical abilities have been frustrated and wasted.

Lady Elliot's death affects all three sisters both individually and in relation to each other. Elizabeth's new position of power enables her to exclude Anne in every possible way, eliminating the possibility of any sympathetic interaction between them. Because of her perception of Anne and her power over her neither sister can be useful to the other – beyond the fact that in Bath Anne makes a convenient fourth at table and can be required to admire, or at least look round, the new house (159). Anne cannot exercise either her nurturing or her practical abilities towards the repellent Elizabeth, but she can care for her younger sister, Mary. She can be a companion to Mary, sympathize with her, tend her and her young children, and offer gentle criticism.

All the same, Lady Elliot's death has weakened this relationship, too, breaking the connection between Anne and Mary when Anne was sent away to school for three years. Moreover, Mary, left from the age of ten largely to whatever guidance Sir Walter and Elizabeth might provide, has adopted some of their values and suffers from "a great deal too much of the Elliot pride" (118), a quite different kind of pride from Anne's fastidious distaste for venal and selfish behaviour. Mary has some sense of what is considered right but Austen most often makes this sense apparent in the blatant contrast between her words and her actions.[11] At the beginning of a letter, she deplores Mrs Harville's behaviour in leaving her children with the Musgroves; at the end of the same letter, she proposes to leave her own sons with their grandparents for weeks. The value of her maternal feelings has already become evident through her announcement to Anne that, because she lacks a mother's sensibilities,

Anne must be the best person to look after Mary's ailing son. As ever in Austen's fiction, feeling is an insufficient guide and caring is more a matter of behaviour than of emotion.[12] In the permanent absence of her mother and the temporary absence of Anne, and without the natural intelligence of either woman, Mary, though "good natured enough" (118) and with capacity for "great good humour and excellent spirits" (75), has acquired much of the folly of her father and eldest sister.

The mother's death and the ensuing changes in household arrangements give Elizabeth too great a sense of her own importance and too little sense of her responsibilities. Mary, bereaved at the age of ten, grows up without resilience, resources or self-knowledge. Anne, who has lost her only intellectual and moral equal in the family, is left with all the required talents for social and domestic responsibility and little opportunity for exercising them until the satisfying closing of the narrative.

* * *

"The real evils […] of Emma's situation were the power of having rather too much of her own way, and a disposition to think a little too well of herself" (55). These words apply to Elizabeth Elliot, too, only without the qualifications: Elizabeth has much too much of her own way and thinks far too well of herself. Elizabeth sees her role as mistress of her father's house in terms of its power and prestige. So does Emma Woodhouse, but for Emma this role is also a matter of responsibility – pleasurable responsibility, no doubt, given Emma's active spirit, but responsibility nevertheless. As her father's most constant companion, Elizabeth only fosters in Sir Walter the vanity, social snobbery and extravagance that she cannot see as faults, given that she shares them. Emma, on the other hand, who does not much resemble her father, does her best to manage his weaknesses and to contain his irrational fears and anxieties. In both cases the loss of the mother (and in Emma's case the early marriage of her elder sister) leads them into over-confidence by giving them power, prestige and a measure of freedom too early: Elizabeth is sixteen, Emma twelve years old when they take charge of their respective households.[13] This over-confidence in turn blinds them to the proper claims of other people. With Elizabeth, this blindness permanently affects her relationships with everyone, even her father. With Emma, it extends only to those who are neither close friends nor family members and her eyes gradually open during the course of the novel.

A more telling comparison is that between Emma and Anne Elliot. Anne suffers emotionally because she has no power and her usefulness is rejected. Emma suffers morally because she has both power and real domestic usefulness. In *Emma*, the mother's death, placing her in a position of power without control, is a practical and ethical rather than an emotional concern as it is in *Persuasion*. Mrs Woodhouse is notably far more absent from the text than is either Lady Elliot or even Mrs Tilney, another significant dead mother, who is present at Northanger Abbey in the imagination of Catherine Morland as well as in the grief of Eleanor Tilney and in her uncomfortable position as the powerless mistress of the house.[14] While the sadness of Lady Elliot's story and Anne's multiple losses permeates much of *Persuasion*, Mrs Woodhouse's absence does nothing to diminish the exuberant atmosphere of *Emma*. All that remains of her for Emma herself is pleasant enough, being just "an indistinct remembrance of her caresses" (55). Only Mr Knightley recognizes the full effects of Emma's loss of her mother: "'In her mother [Emma] lost the only person able to cope with her. She inherits her mother's talents and must have been under subjection to her,'" he tells Mrs Weston (80), who in her days as Miss Taylor had been unable, from her position as governess as well as through her unassertive character, to exert the kind of authority that Emma needed and still needs, according to Mr Knightley. Since her mother's death Miss Taylor has given her the companionship and emotional support that she needs, so that Emma is not conscious of any lack of maternal care. When, at the beginning of the novel, she is again deprived of a mother figure as Miss Taylor marries, the narrative begins.[15]

The fact that "'she inherits her mother's talents'" has of course other implications beyond those Mr Knightley mentions in this conversation. Most are positive. Like Anne Elliot, Emma has not only her mother's intelligence but also her practical ability. Again like Anne, she has a strong sense of the proper responsibilities of the mistress of a large house and of her obligations to the surrounding community, visiting the poor and offering hospitality to her less privileged neighbours. Emma's generosity and sense of community is expressed in the important part played by food in this novel, a far larger part in *Emma* than in any of Austen's other novels.[16] Food in *Emma*, the suppers, the dinners, the presents of soup and pork and apples, is always part of a social interaction, a gift or an element in hospitality, and Emma herself is usually the giver.

Through Emma's domestic and social activities and responsibilities Austen communicates her energy and zest for life as well as her generosity and intelligence. Emma provides abundantly and considerately for her guests, doing her best to make sure that her father's misguided care for their health does not lead to their "unwilling self-denial" (207) – although in Emma's absence old Mrs Bates is forced to go without the asparagus and sweetbreads that she likes so much (291). She offers hospitality as far as she can, given her father's preference for quiet and early hours, making sure, for instance, that Mr Knightley dines with them as soon as the London Knightleys arrive at

Hartfield and giving a dinner party for the Eltons as is due to a bridal pair. In these activities, genuine goodwill is combined with justifiable pride in her own competence and the occasional complacency:

> With a spirit that yet was never indifferent to the credit of doing every thing well and attentively, with the real goodwill of a mind delighted with its own ideas, did she then do all the honours of the meal and help and recommend the minced chicken and scalloped oysters with an urgency that she knew would be acceptable to the early hours and civil scruples of her guests. (70)

Austen's language here tellingly combines references to Emma's genuinely charitable feelings and her self-esteem, her concern with "credit" and her "real goodwill." Emma is both thoughtful for her guests and pleased with herself for being so thoughtful. Inheriting her mother's talents, talents that both her father and sister lack, she is both genuinely superior and a little too aware of her own superiority.

If both parents influence Emma's over-confidence, her mother through her absence and her father through his feebleness, so does the sister who, as the elder, should be her peer or her superior. Isabella's early marriage leaves Emma at the age of twelve as virtual head of the household with all the added privileges of that position. Equally important, Isabella's slowness and diffidence inevitably make Emma, from an early age, conscious of her own quick wits and superior competence. Just as in *Persuasion* Elizabeth's position and assertive personality foster Anne's sadness, so Isabella's abdication from her position and her unassertive personality foster Emma's unrealistic view of her own powers. The elder sister clearly affects the development of the younger: if the younger affects the elder – if Elizabeth is jealous of Anne's closeness to her mother as her outright hostility to Anne might suggest, or if Isabella marries early partly to move into a position where she is the unrivalled lady of the house – that effect is suggested in the gentlest possible fashion.

Anne and Elizabeth have nothing in common except a name and a home. Emma and Isabella, however, share something of great importance to the narrative, namely strong family affection. Isabella is "so tenderly attached to her father and sister" that, without the even "higher ties" to her husband and children, "warmer love" would seem impossible (122). Emma, too, imagines for much of the narrative that all her emotional needs can be met within her family. It is Emma's affection for her sister that makes her especially alert to "the little injuries to Isabella" inflicted by her irritable husband, though Isabella herself never notices them (122). Her love extends to Isabella's children and characteristically it is an active love: Austen represents her as playing with baby

Emma, making letter-cards for her little nephews and repeatedly telling them the story of Harriet and the gypsies. Terry Castle asserts that "throughout *Emma* infants and children will figure as living emblems of the world beyond the self" (xvii). Children need care, and *Emma* is indubitably about the need for care in human interactions. From the beginning of the narrative, Emma herself is skilled in such care and she becomes more skilled as it progresses, and she moves into the world beyond the self and the family. Both her mother's absence and her mother's legacy contribute to Emma's initial complacency as well as to her development away from it.

* * *

Bereaved as they are of their mothers, both Anne Elliot and Emma Woodhouse have kindly but inadequate substitutes: Lady Russell is over-prudent and lacks insight, while Mrs Weston is too complaisant and lacks authority. Fanny Price has a positive redundancy of inadequate mother-figures. The two Mansfield aunts who so casually take on the maternal role naturally affect Fanny's sense of herself and her possible usefulness, but it is largely through Fanny's actual mother that Austen explores concepts of domestic usefulness and exertion in *Mansfield Park*. Both the absence of her mother, when Fanny is taken away to Mansfield, and the presence of her mother, when Fanny returns to Portsmouth, arouse in the daughter anxieties about her own role and her own usefulness.

Taken from her own home at the age of ten, Fanny is marginalized for the next eight years as a poor relation at Mansfield, just as Anne is marginalized at Kellynch as an unwanted sister and daughter, and, as with Anne, the predictable result is despondency. In her own home, poor and ill-run though it was, as the eldest daughter in a large family, Fanny was useful, important to her brothers and sisters as "playfellow, instructress, and nurse" (45). At Mansfield Park, however, she has no function beyond that of a recipient of charity and condescension. Often the object of contempt or ridicule, she seems "'dependent, helpless, friendless, neglected, forgotten'" (304). However, these are the words of Henry Crawford, who exaggerates a little in his pleasure at the favour he is conferring on Fanny by loving her. For as she grows older, Fanny is by no means "helpless" or "friendless." Edmund is always her friend and she is useful to her aunt Bertram if only as a companion. While the activities of a companion to such a woman are neither demanding nor intrinsically rewarding she has the emotional recompense of Lady Bertram's affection and dependence on her and a comforting sense of her own usefulness.

The word "useful" and its cognates recur throughout *Mansfield Park*, most often as applied to Fanny and the other Price children. As Austen's narrative moves to the Prices' home in Portsmouth it extends its concern with questions of obligations and usefulness. One of Fanny's first thoughts when she hears about the proposed visit is of her usefulness to her mother, which she sees as a way of winning love. On her arrival she starts work almost immediately on her brother Sam's naval outfit, being "very anxious to be useful" (392); having managed to get it half ready in time she has "great pleasure in feeling her usefulness" (392). William's first response to the news of Fanny's visit is much like her own – Fanny will be useful:

> "I do not know how it is," said he, "but we seem to want some of your nice ways and orderliness at my father's. The house is always in confusion. You will set things going in a better way, I am sure. You will tell my mother how it all ought to be, and you will be so useful to Susan and you will teach Betsy, and make the boys love and mind you. How right and comfortable it will all be." (429)

The optimistic William oversimplifies the situation, misjudging the characters involved. While Fanny is certainly "useful to Susan," she cannot "teach Betsy," who has been "trained up to think the alphabet her greatest enemy" (393) and is accustomed to doing just what she likes. Moreover, Fanny lacks the confidence to tell anyone, let alone her own mother, "how it all ought to be," even if Mrs Price were prepared to listen to and follow her daughter's advice. The domestic confusion that disturbs William, the product of comparative poverty, too many children and Mrs Price's incompetence, is not so easily remedied.

Fanny's harsh judgment of her mother's failings is certainly in part an emotional response to Mrs Price's indifference to her elder daughters, but it is also based on recognition of her mother's real domestic inadequacies. Fanny perceives her as

> a partial, ill-judging parent, a dawdle, a slattern, who neither taught nor restrained her children, whose house was the scene of mismanagement and discomfort from beginning to end, and who had no talent, no conversation, no affection towards herself, no curiosity to know her better, no desire of her friendship, and no inclination for her company that could lessen her sense of such feelings. (392)

Fanny's view, censorious though it may be, is supported by the narrative. Though Mrs Price is expecting William and Fanny's arrival after the long journey from Mansfield in "the dirty month of February," she has neither prepared a meal for them nor made sure of a good fire, and despite her general preference for boys and particular partiality to William, she has forgotten to alter William's uniform waistcoat, while Sam's naval outfit is only half completed and then as a result of Fanny's working "early and late, with perseverance and great dispatch" (392). Mrs Price's maternal affection is, like Mary Musgrove's, merely a matter of "the instinct of nature" (391) or what Mary Wollstonecraft in her account of maternal affection calls "brutish" (290).

Mrs Price's domestic and maternal failings, and Fanny's absence in Northamptonshire have changed the relationships between the Price children. Susan has had to take over the difficult role of eldest daughter in a chaotic and over-populated household. Initially Fanny is disturbed by Susan's defensive attitude and the overbearing treatment of the younger children so often adopted by older siblings to their juniors. Eventually, though, she comes not only to understand but also to admire Susan's behaviour and finally to love Susan herself. Fanny's admiration for her sister, like her low opinion of their mother, is based largely on standards of domestic competence. She shows admirable self-knowledge in comparing herself to her sister:

> Susan saw much that was wrong at home, and wanted to set it right. That a girl of fourteen, acting only on her own unassisted reason, should err in the method of reform, was not wonderful; and Fanny soon became more disposed to admire the natural light of the mind which could so early distinguish justly, than to censure severely the faults of conduct to which it led. Susan was only acting on the same truths, and pursuing the same system, which her own judgment acknowledged, but which her own more supine and yielding temper would have shrunk from asserting. Susan tried to be useful, where *she* could only have gone away and cried; and that Susan was useful she could perceive. (397 – Austen's emphasis)

Through the domestic confusion of the Price household, Austen explores the necessity for traditional female usefulness and exertion, showing how different kinds of women deal with domestic responsibilities. The narrator informs us that, while the indolent Mrs Price might have done quite as well as Lady Bertram as a lady of leisure, the active Mrs Norris would have done far better at managing a large household on a small income (391–2).[17] And while, with all her intelligence and desire to help, Fanny might merely have cried in face of the domestic difficulties caused by Mrs Price's inadequacies, Susan soldiers on.

Miserable though Fanny is in Portsmouth, it is here that she begins to regain a sense of purpose, independence and capacity to act, showing a degree of initiative that was never required of her at Mansfield. She sews busily for Sam, and though she is unaccustomed to spending money and afraid of interference, buys the silver knife that ends the dispute between Susan and Betsy. She subscribes to a circulating library and begins to educate Susan. And through this activity the two elder sisters, deprived as they are of parental affection, are drawn together, with Fanny taking on the maternal role of teacher and advisor:

> Fanny was [Susan's] oracle. Fanny's explanations and remarks were a most important addition to every essay, or every chapter of history. What Fanny told her of former times, dwelt more in her mind than the pages of Goldsmith; and she paid her sister the compliment of preferring her style to that of any printed author. (418)

The repetition of Fanny's name in this passage underlines the sense of Susan's growing attachment to her elder sister.

The dynamic between Fanny and Susan repeats the dynamic between William and Fanny: as a child, Fanny turned to her elder brother for affection and support, as "her constant companion and friend; her advocate with her mother […] in every distress" (46), just as Susan turns to Fanny. In return, she becomes "the first object of his love" (246). The mother's inadequacy, making brothers and sisters dependent on each other for help and affection, draws them closer together.

Fanny imagines her return to Mansfield, as she had imagined her visit to Portsmouth, in terms of usefulness. In her concern over Tom's illness, her greatest desire is to help: "Could she have been at home, she might have been of service to every creature in the house. She felt that she must have been of use to all. To all she must have saved some trouble of head or hand" (431). Throughout the novel, usefulness is represented not only as a virtue but also as a pleasure and a comfort. Like Edmund, Fanny finds comfort in her sense of usefulness on their return to Mansfield after Maria's elopement. Edmund tries "to bury his own feelings" by caring for Tom, while Fanny feels that "she could never do enough for one who seemed so much to want her" as her aunt Bertram (447). Part of the education of Sir Thomas Bertram, a major concern of the last chapter of the novel, is the usefulness of the Price children:

> In [Susan's] usefulness, in Fanny's excellence, in William's good conduct and rising fame, and in the general well-doing and success of the other members of the family, all assisting each other and doing credit to his countenance and aid, Sir Thomas saw repeated, and for ever repeated reason to rejoice in what he had done for them all, and acknowledge the advantages of early hardship and discipline and the consciousness of being born to struggle and endure. (467–8)

Even the self-indulgent Henry Crawford hankers a little after the brave and useful life of a sailor.

In fact, it is Henry Crawford who, in thoughtlessly quoting the best-known biblical passage concerning the "virtuous woman" (Proverbs 31.10) indicates the principled basis of the sense of domestic usefulness put forward in *Mansfield Park*. Characteristically, Henry is merely being playful and his play is more than a little malicious, for when he announces "'I do not like to eat the bread of idleness,'" the exertion he proposes for himself is to make Fanny Price in love with him (242). However, he is, perhaps unconsciously, quoting serious words – the ending of the Book of Proverbs: "She looketh well to the ways of her household and eateth not the bread of idleness" (31.27), part of a long passage about the value and beauty of domestic industry and care.[18] While Fanny would never claim to have "a price far above rubies" (Proverbs 31.10), her family name has perhaps some such significance, and her sense of proper feminine virtue and activity is in the tradition of this passage. Everything about Fanny suggests a love of the concept of home and domestic usefulness. Even her pleasure in the East Room, her own domain, is largely a love for the one domestic space in which she can exercise her need to nurture and to express affection, even if the recipients of her care are only her plants and the expression of affection is merely a drawing of William's ship pinned to the wall. When she marries Edmund and goes off to Thornton Lacey, part of the pleasure of the ending is similar to that in *Persuasion*. Not only does the heroine have the man she wants; she also has the scope she needs to exercise her domestic taste and talents.

* * *

The relationship between Fanny and Susan Price is shaped by the incompetence and indifference of their mother. Mrs Dashwood in *Sense and Sensibility* is anything but indifferent; nor is she precisely incompetent. No parent can be perfect, however, and Mrs Dashwood's flaws as a parent, like the more serious deficiencies of Mrs Price, help shape the relationship between her elder daughters. In Chapter Two, I discussed how the Dashwoods can and cannot be seen as a dysfunctional family. Here I focus on a specific and practical aspect of this affectionate mother's behaviour and its effect on domestic arrangements and family interactions. Mrs Dashwood comes to acknowledge her own emotional "imprudence" in relation to Marianne's unhappy love for Willoughby (355). Her practical imprudence also affects the love between Marianne and Elinor, a love that Austen places at the centre of this novel.[19]

The series of deaths that trigger the action of *Sense and Sensibility* expose the Dashwood sisters and their mother to difficulties they had not faced before. Without a father or a responsible brother in the traditional role of defender, the sisters are vulnerable to young men such as Edward and Willoughby who cannot or will not explain their intentions. The loss of prestige and money that follows the loss of husband, father and home exposes them to new social difficulties as well as to material problems. The death of the father changes the relations of mother and daughters and the mother's response to her new situation further changes the relations between the sisters. In the first chapter of *Sense and Sensibility*, which establishes these drastic changes, the narrator immediately comments on Mrs Dashwood's "eagerness of mind" and associates it with possible "imprudence" (44) and impracticality. This characteristic pushes her eldest daughter into becoming "the counselor of her mother" (44), a reversal of roles that makes Elinor appear more practical and prudent than might otherwise seem either natural or attractive at the age of nineteen.[20] Domestic responsibilities include material and social concerns that, at least temporarily, Mrs Dashwood cannot or does not address.

Mrs Dashwood, overcome by the emotional impact of her husband's death, fails to grasp fully its financial implications. It is Elinor who, despite her own grief, must take a practical approach to their severely reduced income, rejecting several houses as too expensive to run, limiting to three the number of servants they take to Barton Cottage, advising the sale of the family carriage and so on. Mrs Dashwood is no Elizabeth Elliot or Mrs Bennet – she understands the importance of financial principles and financial independence, and refuses hospitality that she cannot afford to return (77). However, she is generally indifferent to practical matters and this romantic indifference influences Marianne, encouraging her in a kind of idealistic and thoughtless disdain for such mundane concerns. She claims that money – "beyond a mere competence" – has nothing to do with happiness, yet Marianne's idea of "a mere competence" turns out to exceed, even double, Elinor's idea of wealth (122).

The concept of prudence includes normative social interactions as well as material concerns. It is again Elinor who, often with considerable emotional effort, exercises social as well as financial prudence. For reasons of convenience as well as of kindliness, families and individuals are expected to maintain amicable relations with their neighbours and the community at large. The Dashwoods individually and communally have social obligations to the Middletons, the Palmers and Mrs Jennings, however unsympathetic they may find them. Marianne, however, refuses to acknowledge these obligations. Because Mrs Dashwood is unwilling to control Marianne in any way, it is Elinor rather than her mother who has a "plan of general civility" with regard to Marianne (124), a plan that Marianne rejects entirely for a long time. Even the burden of keeping up proper family relationships is left to Elinor, and given the grasping and narrow-minded nature of her half-brother and, more particularly, his wife, this is indeed a burden.

Altogether, Mrs Dashwood's avoidance of practical responsibilities and concentration on the emotional and intellectual aspects of family life leave Elinor with all the less sympathetic and more repressive parental tasks in regard to Marianne. She is obliged to remind Marianne of the need for thrift and make her understand that Willoughby's proposed gift of a horse would involve the family in unwarrantable expense. She must attempt to persuade Marianne to behave civilly to people as cold-hearted as Lady Middleton and Fanny Dashwood, as mindlessly cheerful as Charlotte Palmer and Sir John Middleton and as vulgar as Mrs Jennings. For someone as young and as idealistically concerned with truth and intellectual values as Marianne, Elinor's insistence on the importance of money and of "telling lies when politeness required it" (149–50) is distasteful and perhaps especially distasteful as coming from a sibling. Mrs Dashwood, in treating the child who so resembles her as a sister rather than as a daughter, unintentionally places Elinor in the unenviable position of the repressive mother.

Given the contrasting roles the two sisters have taken on – Elinor parentally repressive, Marianne insistently expressive – the occasional friction between the two is unsurprising, despite their undoubted mutual affection and their common tastes and values.[21] Both sisters can sound quite acid when addressing each other. Because of Elinor's belief in the need for self-control, Marianne tends to underestimate her sister's emotional capacity and to oppose her concepts of good behaviour. She wilfully perverts her sister's "doctrine" of civility: "'I thought our judgments were given to us merely to be subservient to our neighbours,'" she says to Elinor ironically (124). Elinor for her part combines teasing her sister for excessive openness about her affections and preferences with reproof of Marianne. For much of the early part of the novel, conversations between Elinor and Marianne tend to adopt a pattern of quasi-parental chiding and quasi-filial rebuttal.

Eventually it is Elinor's behaviour, not her words, that speaks to Marianne. Only when she learns at last of Edward's engagement to Lucy Steele does Marianne gradually begin to understand the intensity of Elinor's suffering and the quality of her behaviour. In a scene as crucial to the relations between the two sisters as Marianne's confession to Elinor of Willoughby's treachery, and almost as painful, Elinor explains her silence about the engagement in terms of family love, the love that throughout the narrative is demonstrably the mainspring of Elinor's actions. She tells Marianne: "'I did not love only him; – and while the comfort of others was dear to me I was glad to spare them from knowing how much I felt'" (276). While Marianne certainly loves her mother and her sisters, she has in her adherence to the precepts of sensibility perhaps not rated this habitual family love as highly as the romantic sexual passion she feels for Willoughby, a kind of love with much more literary prestige. Accordingly, her first response to Elinor's assertion about family love indicates her belief that, given her behaviour, Elinor cannot have cared much for Edward.

Elinor, driven to defend herself for once, gives a catalogue of her sufferings – from the Ferrars family's hostility, from Lucy's triumphant malice, and from her own sense of Edward's unhappiness in his mistaken engagement. Through the broken speech patterns, quite untypical of this normally controlled and articulate young woman, Austen indicates the strength of Elinor's feelings:

> And all this has been going on at a time when, as you know too well, it has not been my only unhappiness. – If you can think me capable of ever feeling – surely you may suppose that I have suffered *now*. The composure of mind with which I have brought myself at present to consider the matter, the consolation that I have been willing to admit, have been the effect of constant and painful exertion; – they did not spring up of themselves; – they did not occur to relieve my spirits at first – No, Marianne, – *Then* if I had not been bound to silence, perhaps nothing could have kept me entirely – not even what I owed to my dearest friends – from openly shewing that I was *very* unhappy. (277 – Austen's emphases)

The belated realization of Elinor's sufferings compels Marianne to believe that her sister's behaviour springs not from indifference but from love and active principle: she begins to grasp, intellectually if not at first emotionally, the connection between love and exertion. The contrast between her own behaviour and Elinor's initiates a slow and painful change.[22] At first she suffers "only the torture of penitence without the hope of amendment" (283), but penitence is of course, in the Christian ethics by which Austen lived and wrote, the necessary first step towards a new life.[23]

Through her sister Marianne comes to realize the duty of avoiding giving pain to others. She has finally understood both the basis in charity of Elinor's insistence on civility – "general complaisance" and "particular gratitude" – and the fact that such charity, whether "duty" or "friendship," involves exertion:

> Had I died, – in what peculiar misery should I have left you, my nurse, my friend, my sister! – […] you above all, above my mother, had been wronged by me. I, and I only, knew your heart and its sorrows; yet to what did it influence me? – not to any compassion that could benefit you or myself. – Your example was before me: but to what avail? Was I more considerate of you and your comfort? Did I imitate your forbearance or lessen your restraints by taking any part in those offices of general

complaisance or particular gratitude which you had hitherto been left to discharge alone? – No: – not less when I knew you to be unhappy than when I had believed you at ease, did I turn away from every exertion of duty or friendship, scarcely allowing sorrow to exist but within me […] leaving you, for whom I professed an unbounded affection, to be miserable for my sake. (350–51)

In recognizing the basis of Elinor's behaviour in affection, Marianne comes to understand her own behaviour as a failure of affection – a failure indeed of sensibility. Marianne learns through her own pain and through Elinor's example what might have been acquired more easily from her mother's advice, as Mrs Dashwood herself finally acknowledges. When Marianne asserts that she has nothing to regret except her own folly, her mother returns, "rather say your mother's imprudence […] *She* must be answerable" (355). Mrs Dashwood's "imprudence" included an avoidance of practical obligations and of the social education of Marianne, as well as the more obvious imprudence involved in her excessive trust of Willoughby.

In the new family situation that follows the death of the father Elinor's reaction to her widowed mother's inevitable shortcomings as sole parent polarizes the two sisters for a time: Elinor occasionally comes to represent sense (for Marianne) and Marianne occasionally comes to represent sensibility (for Elinor). Austen though presents all three women as complex and highly intelligent. As the sisters adjust their relationship and their understanding of each other and of themselves, so the mother adjusts her understanding of her new domestic role.

***

The absence of just two novels from this discussion deserves some comment. The case of *Northanger Abbey* is clear enough: the novel is concerned with Catherine's formation outside her family. Mrs Morland is evidently an excellent mother and her realistic approach to domestic life is suggested by her initial response to Catherine's engagement: "'Catherine would make a sad heedless young housekeeper to be sure,' was her mother's foreboding remark; but quick was the consolation of there being nothing like practice" (237).[24] The affectionate tranquillity of Catherine's home at Fullerton, however, acts only as a "common life" frame to the narrative of her career as a "heroine."

Mrs Bennet – who greets *her* daughter's engagement with "ten thousand a year! Oh Lord! What will become of me, I shall go distracted!" (377) – is quite a different matter from Mrs Morland and Longbourn is more central to *Pride and Prejudice* than Fullerton is to *Northanger Abbey*. Mrs Bennet's character affects the relations of her elder daughters just as Mrs Dashwood affects Marianne and Elinor though in a very different way. The narrator introduces her abruptly as "a woman of mean understanding, little information and an uncertain temper" (45). Given their abilities, Jane and Elizabeth inevitably differentiate themselves from such a mother in every possible way. In this they are successful: Darcy tells Elizabeth that the difference between their conduct and that of the rest of the family is generally known and praised as "honourable to the sense and disposition of both" (218). This difference makes the two sisters highly dependent on each other and Elizabeth turns to her elder sister as to a mother: Jane is indeed "a most beloved sister" (212).

Yet *Pride and Prejudice* is far less domestic in its concerns than the four novels discussed here. In fact the most domestic figure in the novel is Charlotte Collins, happy, despite her husband, with "her home and her housekeeping, her parish and her poultry" (233). No such concerns touch either Jane or Elizabeth. Austen establishes that they both are capable of active caring, yet part of the pleasurable "light & bright & sparkling" quality of the novel, of which Austen playfully complains (*Letters* 203) is *Pride and Prejudice*'s comparative lack of concern with "usefulness and exertion." The sense of the importance of domestic competence and domestic activity to women's lives is a lesser concern in Austen's most enduringly popular novel.

Part II

FATHERS AND DAUGHTERS

INTRODUCTION

Both the nature of the relationship between father and daughter and the strong contrast between them are crucial in various ways in Austen's last four novels. Although Mr Bennet is a careless father, Elizabeth and her father clearly love each other and continue to relish each other's company. Sir Thomas Bertram's absence is necessary for the plot of *Mansfield Park*, but the significance of his absence to his family, and especially his daughters, arises from the repression of his presence, so that Fanny Price's "habitual dread" (194) of him can only gradually develop into affection, as she becomes eventually "the daughter he wanted" (467). Mr Woodhouse is in his way as poor a parent as Mr Bennet, but Emma Woodhouse, the most considerate of daughters, ends as she began, caring for him in his own home. Only in *Persuasion* is the relationship between father and daughter virtually loveless, and this lovelessness is significant in itself. As for the contrasts between father and daughter, in the three novels written at Chawton, *Mansfield Park*, *Emma* and *Persuasion*, Austen represents the father figure as a foil for its heroine in regard to issues that are central to the novel's ethical concerns.[1] These strong contrasts between young women and older and more powerful men in the Chawton novels are the subject of Part II of this book.[2]

***

Mr Bennet is the first developed father figure in Jane Austen's novels. His daughter Elizabeth's resemblance to him is striking. Both father and daughter are clever, articulate and critical, and Elizabeth has learned or inherited from her father the pleasure of laughing at other people's "follies and nonsense, whims and inconsistencies" (92). Elizabeth loves her father, but recognizes the harm he causes through his unwillingness either to exert himself or to fulfil his responsibilities towards his wife and daughters, moral, behavioural or financial. In contrast, Elizabeth herself faces her family responsibilities, caring for Jane when she is ill at Netherfield, attempting to control the behaviour of Lydia and Kitty, discouraging her father from allowing Lydia's disastrous visit to

Brighton and helping Jane care for her mother after Lydia's elopement. While Mr Bennet characteristically retreats to his library, Elizabeth moves outwards to Meryton and Netherfield and then to London, Kent and Derbyshire.

Superior though she is to her father, Elizabeth is, as I said, recognizably his daughter. In the three novels that follow *Pride and Prejudice* – *Mansfield Park*, *Emma* and *Persuasion* – the contrast between the heroine and her father or father-figure becomes more extreme, and, as with Elizabeth, the difference is invariably and greatly to the heroine's advantage. The following chapters examine these contrasts in relation to issues of central importance to the novels in question. While Sir Thomas Bertram is easily swayed by expediency and by material motives, Fanny Price is immoveable in her principles. This contrast is discussed in Chapter Four, which argues that *Mansfield Park* is woven through with a concern about attitudes to money, an issue articulated partly through the contrast between Sir Thomas and Fanny. The spoken word, through which Emma shines as her father can never, would never, hope to do, is even more important in *Emma* than in any other of these novels. In *Emma*, Austen focuses upon the role of speech and silence in social interactions – and the point here is that Mr Woodhouse, living in a world closed both by his lack of intelligence and his cushioned way of life, is a non-player.[3] Chapter Five deals with the ethics of speech and silence in *Emma*. In *Persuasion*, Anne Elliot is as affectionate and helpful as Sir Walter Elliot is cold and self-indulgent. The relation between Anne's responsiveness and Sir Walter's narcissism is embodied in their contrasting attitudes to personal appearance, the subject of Chapter Six. The contrasts involved in all three novels undermine some of the most common stereotypes of gender at the period. The physically timid Fanny shows a moral courage that Sir Thomas lacks, Emma is far cleverer than her father, Anne far less vain than hers.

Austen's contrasts between fathers and daughters in these novels are, of course, neither complete nor simplistic. Fanny's standards are more akin to Sir Thomas's than to any other major character in *Mansfield Park* apart from Edmund.[4] Similarly Emma shares a degree of self-importance with the father who thinks she is perfect. This small degree of resemblance between father and daughter is harmful: Robert Miles writes, "in *Emma* […] the father's weakness becomes the daughter's headlong rush into error" (34).[5] Yet Mr Woodhouse's weaknesses also develop in Emma an incipient consideration and tolerance she rarely shows elsewhere. And while Anne Elliot's sense of her father's inadequacies constantly pains and embarrasses her, this distant relationship gives her an independence that Emma Woodhouse denies herself.

Austen is working both within and beyond a fictional tradition in these contrasted pairs of fathers and daughters. Mary Waldron argues that in the eighteenth century "novelists had largely felt it incumbent upon them to support the conduct-book standard – the success of the heroine most often lay in her own efforts to do right, usually in opposition to traditional authority figures, at the same time as endorsing supposed external norms of proper submission" (41). On the other hand, Patricia Meyer Spacks asserts that "eighteenth century novels, especially novels about women, explained youthful virtue as largely the consequence of adult guidance" ("Muted Discord" 164). These critics seem to be arguing on the basis of a different selection of eighteenth-century texts, so that both their arguments have a partial validity. What their differing views confirm is the existence of a fictional tradition that evaluates the role of the authority figure in relation to the moral activity and development of the heroine. Tellingly, Austen's fiction aligns itself to that element of the tradition that Waldron discusses, of the necessary opposition to traditional authority figures, while her heroines' adherence to "supposed external norms of proper submission" is largely a matter of common courtesy and a modification of the commandment to "honor thy father and thy mother" – as far as is possible, Anne Elliot might add silently. Her attitude to Sir Walter may amount to what Julia Prewitt Brown calls "resigned contempt" (*Jane Austen* 130), but she scrupulously observes the conventions of filial behaviour.

The relation between father and daughter in these novels underlines the fact that family hierarchies based on the socially recognized distinctions of power, property and convention are very different from those based on merit. The fathers, all wealthy landowners, are markedly inferior to some of their daughters or foster-daughters. Judith Wilt exaggerates only a little when she observes, commenting on Austen's relation to the Gothic novel,

> Austen's live fathers – the sarcastic and ineffectual Mr Bennet of *Pride and Prejudice*, the affable but selfish Sir Thomas Price [*sic*] of *Mansfield Park*, *Emma*'s delicate and tyrannical Mr Woodhouse, *Persuasion*'s vain and obtuse Sir Walter Elliot – are as willful and threatening to their daughters' happiness as Montoni [of *The Mysteries of Udolpho*] is to his niece. (129)

These three contrasting pairs of fathers and daughters show Austen challenging both traditional authority relations and traditional assumptions about gender.

Chapter Four

MONEY, MORALS AND *MANSFIELD PARK*

Even more than Jane Austen's other novels, *Mansfield Park* hinges from beginning to end on the relations between the different generations of one family.[1] Its first pages give the marital arrangements of the parents of the central characters; its last pages establish a new order of relations between parents and children, and hint at a future generation at Mansfield Parsonage.[2] Virtually every one of these intergenerational relationships is harmful in one way or another.[3] Sir Thomas Bertram unintentionally alienates his children and Lady Bertram neglects them. Mrs Norris merely flatters and indulges them. Mrs Rushworth's blind worship of that "very stupid fellow," her son, does nothing to increase his capacities (68). Henry Crawford is corrupted by his uncle, the Admiral, and Mary Crawford is coarsened by the Admiral's unhappy and mercenary wife. Susan Price is embittered and Betsy Price spoilt by their mother's unfair treatment of them.

As for Fanny Price, the novel's heroine, she has an over-abundance of parent-figures and is mistreated to varying degrees by all of them. Her mother and father are indifferent to her, her uncle terrifies her, her aunt Bertram exploits her, while literally every speech that Mrs Norris addresses to or at Fanny inflicts some wound, major or minor. Fanny's "creepmouse" (166) qualities and her almost crippling desire to oblige and to be useful clearly result from this combination of coldness and perpetual harassment. Yet for all the abuse, intentional and unintentional, that she suffers at Mansfield Park, Fanny loves the place and appears finally as the moral heir to its owner, Sir Thomas. She is the appropriate figure to be bringing a new generation to Mansfield. In this chapter I examine how Fanny both resembles and differs from Sir Thomas, arguing that their most fundamental and significant difference lies in their attitudes towards money, a central concern of this novel.

Sir Thomas and Fanny are in certain ways as much, if not more, like each other as any other pair of characters in the novel. They share a sense of the importance of principles. They both have a sense of duty that involves a readiness for exertion. Sir Thomas acknowledges his obligations to his family and other dependents, however badly he fulfils them. Apart from his usual business on his Northamptonshire estate, his obligations both as father and as landowner involve the long journey to Antigua and protracted stay there, or so he believes. Fanny fulfils her obviously tedious duties as Lady Bertram's companion and is pathetically glad to work for anyone who wants her, sewing costumes for *Lovers' Vows*, getting her brother's outfit ready for sea, "working early and late, with perseverance and great dispatch" (392). Henry Crawford notes that she accepts without question "'that she is not to have a moment at her own command'" (303). Jane Nardin describes her, with a degree of justice, as "Austen's only full-dress portrait of a working woman" ("Leisure" 132).[4]

In most ways, however, Fanny is carefully differentiated from the other inhabitants of Mansfield and above all from Sir Thomas. She is a marginal figure in Mansfield society.[5] She is repeatedly signified by lack: she is small; she has less health, less energy, less good looks, less confidence, less prestige than the rest of the family. She lacks all the material signs of wealth: there is no fire in her room, her bedroom is an attic next to the maids' rooms, she comes to Mansfield with only two sashes and even as a "young lady" seems only to have one evening dress. What she lacks materially is balanced by what she possesses intellectually and morally. Her supersensitivity to other people's feelings and responses – a quality she shares with Anne Elliot, nine years her senior – distinguishes her from the rest of her family as much as does her scanty wardrobe or her delicate health.[6] Fanny is an outsider linguistically as well as in other ways. Of the inhabitants of Mansfield Park, J. L. Burrows notes that

> once Lady Bertram is set aside, the whole matrix shows an unusually high level of correlations among the rest – except for Fanny. In this way [...] the claustral ambience of Mansfield is palpable even in the most commonplace of its linguistic habits. And even here, Fanny stands as isolated as she is in matters of principle and conduct. (89)

Fanny at Mansfield is, to her cost and to her honour, an outsider.

Given her anomalous position at Mansfield, Fanny stands in contrast to every other character, differing from all the other young people in her shyness and reticence, differing from her elders in her total lack of self-confidence. In some ways the most obvious contrast to Fanny is predictably that provided by her rival, Mary Crawford, witty, sophisticated, strikingly pretty, rich and self-confident as she is. Yet the contrast between Fanny and Sir Thomas is even more significant. Austen carefully establishes the distance between Sir Thomas and Fanny. Sir Thomas, as the landowner, is at the centre of the Mansfield Park family, Fanny, the poor cousin, is the most marginalized figure there.[7] Apart from Mr Rushworth, Sir Thomas is the richest member of the circle, Fanny the poorest. He is the most powerful; she is the weakest.

The strength of this contrast underscores relentlessly the fact that poor, weak Fanny is able to live up to her principles, while the rich and powerful Sir Thomas cannot do so.[8] As Elsie Michie writes, "in *Mansfield Park*, Austen acknowledges the way that in a commercial culture even the most virtuous of individuals will be attracted to the pursuit of wealth" (13). Indeed it is perhaps because of his wealth and power that Sir Thomas is willing to compromise. And partly for this reason the treatment of money – or rather of attitudes towards money – is of such especial importance in this novel.

Austen never, in any of her writings, ignores what Alistair Duckworth calls "the mercenary and competitive character of her society" (181), but in *Mansfield Park* she explores with especial thoroughness the dangerous omnipresence of the mercenary. Critics have occasionally viewed her treatment of attitudes towards material gain in this novel as being primarily expressed through the contrast between Mansfield and London, generalizing from Mary Crawford's remark about "the true London maxim, that every thing is to be got with money" (86).[9] Tony Tanner sees the whole narrative as questioning whether "Mansfield [can] cure what has been spoilt by London: or will the products of London finally undermine all that Mansfield strives to perpetuate?" – London being, he argues, "a world governed only by considerations of money" ("Introduction" 16). John Wiltshire, discussing the novel's moral geography, seems to imply a similar position: "the sober and repressive morality of Sir Thomas Bertram, in a part of England associated with Cowper, is deliberately contrasted with the new age, and geography is understood in its ethical and historical dimensions" ("Introduction" 1).[10] True, Fanny comes to think "the influence of London very much at war with all respectable attachments" (431). But in regard to attitudes about money there is no real contrast between Mansfield and London. Mansfield does not need London to teach it avarice, nor do the Bertrams need the Crawfords for such lessons. By the time Maria meets the Crawfords she has already engaged herself to the rich but foolish Mr Rushworth, having apparently decided that "her happiness should centre in a large income" (68), while Tom Bertram has already managed to get himself sufficiently in debt to oblige his father to sell the living of Mansfield. Mrs Norris, too, is already well known for her "love of money" (55). Mansfield and London share a false attitude to money from the beginning of the novel almost to its end.

Austen's Victorian readers, sensitized perhaps by Dickens's vituperations against the obsessive materialism of their "right little, tight little island" (57), seem to have been especially aware of this element in *Mansfield Park*.[11] Charlotte Mary Yonge, for instance, followed her best-selling *The Heir of Redclyffe* with a retelling of *Mansfield Park* – *Heartsease: or the Brother's Wife* (1854).[12] There is no need to dwell on *Heartsease* at any length here. The sole purpose in mentioning this novel is to draw attention to the terms of the title of this chapter – money and morals, and also to the significance in these two concepts in relation to the West Indies, a topic that has been much discussed in other contexts over the last thirty years. Yonge's pious mid nineteenth-century re-writing of *Mansfield Park* elaborates on these subjects in a telling fashion. As in *Mansfield Park* its central family possesses mismanaged properties in the Leeward Islands of the West Indies.[13] The novel involves at least half-a-dozen further instances of gross financial mismanagement, corruption and exploitation, as well as a series of both proposed and actual mercenary marriages (Dunlap 1). Evidently Yonge, an astute, if moralistic, reader,[14] saw Austen's West Indian references as related to the insistent concern with false attitudes towards money in *Mansfield Park* and as an important aspect of its narrative.[15] Some Victorian readers and writers, that is, seem to have been prepared to view Austen's fiction in terms of the morality of material and economic issues. After Yonge, however, these concerns were largely ignored by many of Austen's readers for the next century. Not until the later twentieth century, and especially after the publication of Edward Said's "Jane Austen and Empire" in 1989, was the West Indian question seen as being of much significance.[16] Charlotte Yonge evidently realized that Austen's treatment of the Antiguan connection in *Mansfield Park*, sparse though it is, relates closely to Austen's insistence on the significance of attitudes towards money in this novel.

My concern in the following pages, then, is largely with attitudes towards money and material gain rather than with money in itself. Austen is as clear as ever in this novel about income levels and financial endowments, from the first sentence on, in which we learn that Miss Maria Ward has "only seven thousand pounds," which gives her no claim to such a good match as Sir Thomas Bertram. But what matters is the kind of importance placed on these financial concerns. The first sentences of the novel also indicate rather caustically the relations between feminine attractions, financial negotiations, marriage chances and the nature of relationships. Sir Thomas may be "captivate[d] by Miss Maria Ward"; the older sister, Miss Ward, is "obliged" after half-a-dozen years "to be attached to" the financially not especially desirable Reverend Mr Norris. From the first paragraphs onwards, then, attitudes to money (rather than money itself) are crucial to relations within the family and to the formation of the family.

* * *

"I do not write for such dull Elves/As have not a great deal of Ingenuity themselves," writes Jane Austen (*Letters* 202).[17] Nor does she: we, her readers, need whatever wits we have about us. In the case of Sir Thomas Bertram, for instance, Austen's *Mansfield Park* indicates, without direct statement or comment, that he is a slave-owner;[18] Patricia Rozema's screen adaptation of *Mansfield Park*, with its mournful music, slave-ships and horrendous drawings purloined in part from William Blake,[19] insists loudly on the dark significance of this fact. Rozema, like Blake himself, has a good reason for this insistence, given her negative presentation of Sir Thomas in this adaptation. A (Miramax) filmmaker in 1999, such as Rozema, addresses a multi-national audience unlikely to be especially well-informed about British involvement in slavery. An illustrator and engraver, such as Blake, working in the early 1790s, addresses a British readership torn over the question of slavery.[20] Blake, moreover, was engaged with (or against) a text – John Stedman's *Five Years' Expedition Against the Revolted Negroes of Surinam* – that could be regarded as, at best, ambivalent on the subject.[21] Austen, as a novelist, is working in a different and suppler medium. She is also working after the British abolition of the slave trade and addressing an audience sensitized by decades of abolitionist propaganda, propaganda that continued long after the 1807 abolition of the slave trade in British possessions, as it went on to address the issue of international slave trading and the abolition of slavery itself. More significantly, Austen has a different aesthetic. Her realism is austere: one of her most acute Victorian critics, the novelist Margaret Oliphant, notes that "she was conscientious in her determination to describe only what she knew, and [...] nature aided principle in this singular limitation" ("Miss Austen" 215–16).[22] She chose to write with a peculiar subtlety that demands all the "Ingenuity" of those dullish elves, her twenty-first century readers, insisting, as noted earlier, on the importance of "Nature" and "Probability" in her fiction. Her art – Nancy Armstrong describes it as "minimalist art" (134) – is one of implication, precision and economy.[23]

As Edward Said points out, Austen's references to Antigua are minimal. We learn that Sir Thomas has property on the Leeward Island (36), we gather first that it is not prospering (54, 59) and then that its poor returns demand his presence (61) – a prolonged presence (66). We hear that he returns, thin, tired and weather-beaten (196), anxious to talk about his experiences (196), that Fanny asks him about the slave trade, and that his answer to this question – whatever it may have been – ends the conversation, largely because his own children have no interest in the subject (214). And that's it. These references communicate nothing at all about Sir Thomas's behaviour in Antigua or his opinions and observations about slavery there: he may have been either for the slave trade or, more probably, against it.[24]

In another text these may well have been crucial questions. Here the Antiguan allusions function quite differently. In terms of plot, Sir Thomas, the controlling parent, must absent himself from home for a period long enough to allow his family to entangle themselves with the Crawfords, the Rushworths and Mr Yates. Problems with an Antiguan estate provide a perfectly convincing rationale for such an absence. The colony, like the rest of the British West Indies, was in decline at the period at which *Mansfield Park* is set.[25] "Bankruptcy is universal," wrote Governor Lavington from Antigua in 1805. The British parliament set up three committees studying the economic "distress" of West Indian planters between 1807 and 1808 (Ragatz 309).[26]

In regard to the moral positioning of the character of Sir Thomas, Austen's choice of Antigua has complex implications, as it was the West Indian island on which slaves stood the best chance of comparatively humane treatment. In the years after liberation, it would, according to the historian Lowell Ragatz, be the only one in the Antilles "to eventually extend freedom to its slaves without an initial apprenticeship period"(66–7). Its "negro code" included the right of slaves to trial by jury and "placed no restrictions on manumission" (Perry 240). William Wilberforce in 1791, as John Wiltshire notes, comments on the comparative well-being of the slaves of Antigua, attributing it to the work of Moravian and Methodist missionaries ("Decolonising *Mansfield Park*" 312). Earlier, Janet Schaw, in her West Indian journal, had written of Antigua as "strikingly superior to those of the other [British West Indian] possessions with respect to the privilege accorded" the Africans (92), attributing this, not to the missionary work that naturally interested the Evangelical Wilberforce, but to the comparative rarity of absentee landlords on the island.

Sir Thomas, though, *is* an absentee landlord. Austen's references to Antigua, though sparse, have rich and complex implications, implications of which, given her family connections with Antigua, she can hardly have been unaware.[27] Sir Thomas is a slave-owner, a category common enough amongst English gentlemen, but known through the long-standing and continuing propaganda campaigns of the period as being capable either of comparatively humane behaviour or of "Savage Murder," as Hannah More put it in 1795 ("The Sorrows of Yamba" 498). Austen's more sensitive readers would have been aware of its unsavoury connotations. All the same, Sir Thomas owns slaves on an island known for its comparatively merciful treatment of Africans, while being one of those absentee landlords whose inattention can result in abuses.

The few references to Antigua indicate, with splendid economy, the crucial contradictions and complexities of Sir Thomas's character, which are apparent in all his interactions with other people including his family, and more especially in those interactions in which money or material advantage is concerned. Over material advantage Sir Thomas is ready to compromise while Fanny is uncompromising over moral issues. While poor Fanny for many years finds it difficult to love her uncle, she admires him as possessing a "high sense of honour and decorum" (440). Her admiration is qualified, however, for although she hopes that he will recognize, as "a good man" must, "how wretched and how unpardonable, how hopeless and how wicked it was to marry without affection" (329), she also realizes that she cannot expect such "Romantic delicacy" of feeling in a man who had married his daughter to Mr Rushworth (336). The narrative as a whole questions further Sir Thomas's motivation and behaviour. Sir Thomas may never be entirely motivated by "the sordid lust for gold" that More and many others associate with slave-owners (*Slavery* 127), but that "lust" for material advantage affects in some degree virtually every action he takes and accounts for many of his failings as father and foster father.

The very first information Austen provides about Sir Thomas, apart from his rank and his wealth, communicates the mixed motives that habitually impel him. The narrative voice comments, in relation to his willingness to help his new in-laws, the Prices, "Sir Thomas had interest, which, from principle as well as pride, from a general wish of doing right, and a desire of seeing all that were connected with him in situations of respectability, he would have been glad to exert" (35). Principle and pride, the wish to do right and the wish for enhanced respectability: Austen represents Sir Thomas, then, as being, like most of us, motivated by a combination of moral standards and worldly interest. Nor is Sir Thomas alone among Austen's "good" characters in operating through such a combination of motives: one might consider Lady Russell or Mrs Smith in *Persuasion* in the same terms. Peter Knox-Shaw, writing of *Pride and Prejudice*, observes:

> Like Hume and Smith, Jane Austen upheld a pull me push you idea of motivation: the 'natural virtues' founded in sympathy were one inducement to decency, but the care of self-image was the more familiar goad. So it is that sympathy and pride are twinned as motives. (137)

In the case of Sir Thomas, whose motives, "principle" and "pride," are explicitly twinned, this combination drives his actions throughout the novel. They provide a basis for his fundamental decency but also frequently mislead him. For instance, he conscientiously offers to release his daughter Maria from her engagement to the clownish Mr Rushworth as soon as he perceives her indifference to her future husband. When she refuses this offer, however, he is easily satisfied:

> Too glad to be satisfied perhaps to urge the matter quite so far as his judgement might have dictated to others. It was an alliance he could not have relinquished without pain […] happy to escape the embarrassing

evils of such a rupture, the wonder, the reflections, the reproach that must attend it, happy to secure a marriage which would bring him such an addition of respectability and influence. (217)

He acts, that is, largely out of concern for material and social advantage, half-aware that his judgment is being swayed by these considerations, regarding the marriage as an "alliance" rather than a personal relationship.[28] Later he is forced into full consciousness of the motives and implications of his behaviour and comes to realize, out of painful experience, that in relation to Maria's marriage he has "sacrificed the right to the expedient, and been governed by motives of selfishness and worldly wisdom" (447). These same motives – expediency, selfishness, worldly wisdom – are again at work when he tries to bully Fanny into accepting Henry Crawford. He expects his niece to act as he has acted in regard to his daughter's marriage, not out of affection or principle, but out of consideration of "the advantage or disadvantage of [her] family" (324), advantages that are again basically social and material.[29] He sends Fanny off to Portsmouth under the pretext of "the propriety of seeing her family again," but his "prime motive" is that she should come to value not Henry Crawford himself but the comforts his money would offer her (371).[30] She is sent away in order to learn in the squalor of Portsmouth not the value of married love but rather "the value of a good income" (372).

***

From the first page of this novel onwards, Austen represents most of her characters as activated, like Sir Thomas, by a complex of motives, amongst which material gain usually dominates. Their false attitudes towards money disable them from giving due attention to other people's needs or feelings, numbing their sensitivities in relation to others. She also represents virtually every character in this novel as able, again like Sir Thomas, to veil materialism in the language of duty. Only Fanny takes the language of duty literally, as compelling her to behaviours not necessarily conducive to her own comfort, rather than euphemistically, as disguising selfish choices in socially acceptable moral terms. As a wealthy, independent and powerful male, Sir Thomas is free to treat material gain discreetly, in terms of "respectability and influence," rather than of direct financial advantage. Other characters, especially female characters, lacking the freedom inherent in Sir Thomas's privileged position, must take a more direct view of monetary considerations. The more obvious instances of this form of materialism relate to sex and marriage, the form most likely to affect women. As Edward Copeland, discussing *Mansfield Park*, unsentimentally observes, "the heartbeat of romance lies in a good income"

(*Cambridge Companion* 133). Maria Bertram is in some ways a true daughter of her father, inheriting his weaknesses rather than his strengths. She shares the strong sexual drive that presumably led him to marry the lovely but vacuous Miss Maria Ward, and her ruinous marriage is based in part on a perverted version of his sense of duty:

> Being now in her twenty-first year, Maria Bertram was beginning to think matrimony a duty; and as a marriage with Mr Rushworth would give her the enjoyment of a larger income than her father's [...] by the same rule of moral obligation her evident duty was to marry Mr Rushworth if she could. (38–9)[31]

The evident irony of the narrative voice here makes it impossible to assess how far the language of "duty" and "moral obligation" is intended to approximate to Maria's thought, and how far it reflects more generally on the codes of conduct in relation to marriage that were common among the gentry, pseudo-gentry and the middle-classes. Maria and Maria's society are equally condemned by such a commentary.

Elsewhere, Austen puts similar language directly into the mouths of her characters. Maria Bertram might well have gathered her concept of a woman's duty from that most proper source, her own mother. Lady Bertram, giving Maria's cousin Fanny "almost the only rule of conduct" she will ever receive from her aunt, is quite clear on the morality of marriage: "'You must be aware, Fanny, that it is every young woman's duty to accept such a very unexceptionable offer as this'" (337). Marry for money, as probably (presumably) the former Maria Ward did. Mary Crawford, though she is quite clearly to a huge degree Lady Bertram's intellectual superior, significantly echoes her words: "'It is every body's duty to do as well for themselves [in marriage] as they can'" (296–7), she says: "'every body should marry *as soon as they can do it to advantage*'" (71 – my emphasis). Maria, in engaging herself to a man who, without his twelve thousand a year, "would be a very stupid fellow," according to Edmund (68), "'has done no more than what every young woman would do,'" according to Miss Crawford (131). This confusion of the monetary, the moral and the sexual resounds throughout the novel, through Mary's own voice and through that of most other characters, as well as through the ironies of the narrative voice.[32]

Perhaps the most blatant example of this frank and unquestioning acceptance of the monetary basis of sexual life in the upper and middle classes is another of Mary Crawford's comments on the Bertram / Rushworth marriage. Maria, giving her first party of the London season in "one of the best houses in Wimpole Street," is expected to feel "that she has got her pennyworth for her penny" (390). This expression, which Miss Crawford herself acknowledges as being a "vulgar phrase," makes brutally plain the entirely commercial nature of the transactions between the Rushworths: he has bought her, and she has bought him, or at least his position, with the coin of her body, her "penny": elegant but dreary Wimpole Street and its resplendent parties are merely her "pennyworth" (395). "'Everything is to be got with money'": Mary speaks of this as "'the true London maxim'" (86) and she has inevitably absorbed the values of her culture and her education.[33] Thomas Gisborne, writing in 1797, observes that "popular language indicates the state of popular opinion," and that "'a good match'" for a woman always means that "'in point of precedence, in point of command of finery and money, she is, more or less, a gainer by the bargain" (233–4). Mary echoes with her "vulgar phrase" another piece of "popular language," indicating a similar attitude.

Mary Crawford, as well as being pretty and lively, is evidently highly intelligent, as her conversation shows. She is also capable of sympathy: she shows in her various kindnesses to Fanny "the really good feelings by which she was almost purely governed" (167). But Austen represents Mary Crawford's moral confusion over money – a culturally-conditioned confusion – as dulling both her innate intelligence and her capacity for sympathy, just as Sir Thomas's materialism blunts his principles and makes him less likely to perceive the real needs of other people. Mary Crawford has occasionally been likened to the heroine of *Pride and Prejudice*. Yet it is impossible to think of Elizabeth, who is so distressed by her friend Charlotte Lucas's decision to accept Mr Collins for the sake of a comfortable home, making the remarks about money and marriage that Mary makes.

A typical comment of Mary's arises from her thoughts about the unhappy marriage of her friend, Mrs Fraser: "'she could not do otherwise than accept [Mr Fraser], for he was rich and she had nothing'" (364). Miss Crawford here seems quite oblivious of the fact that she is talking to Fanny Price, who having less than nothing, has, all the same, just refused Mary's rich brother. She could indeed "do otherwise." Though Mary is full of "really good feelings" she is often insensitive to other people's feelings. John Wiltshire argues that she misunderstands Fanny because of Fanny's reluctance to communicate with her (*Body* 97). True enough: Fanny, hopelessly in love with Edmund and painfully conscious of his attraction to Mary, a much more suitable match for him both socially and financially, has good reason to hide her feelings, and better reason to hide them from Mary than from anyone else. But Mary's misunderstandings also indicate a more general lack of awareness of other people's likely feelings. This insensitivity seems to increase with time. A more distasteful example of this growing blindness to other people and their sensibilities is Mary's letter to Fanny enquiring about Tom Bertram's illness – "suicidally self-revelatory," according to Juliet McMaster ("Talkers and Listeners" 80). Mary assumes that Fanny's feelings towards Tom's danger must be identical with her own, and exhorts Fanny not to trouble "to be ashamed of either my feelings or your own" (433), apparently believing Fanny must be as content to see her eldest cousin dead and Edmund the heir in his place as Miss Crawford herself would be.

Mary Crawford, in fact, generalizes so much from her own standards – unsurprisingly, since they are those of most her acquaintance – that she assumes that these standards are, or should be, universal. Her capacity for misjudging her company is plain early on when she assumes that Fanny and Edmund would be amused by her risqué joke about Rears and Vices[34] and would share her views about the tedium of family prayers. This tendency to generalize is especially apparent in her treatment of money. When Edmund Bertram asks her – or states – "'you intend to be very rich,'" her immediate, if half-playful, response is, "'to be sure. Do not you? – Do not we all?'" (227–8). And she soon follows this by jeering at Edmund's declared intention of aspiring merely to "'honesty in the middle state of worldly circumstances'" (220). Austen represents Mary Crawford as being as acquisitive in her own way as Mrs Norris – whom, being perceptive, she seems to dislike – is in hers. In fact, Mrs Norris, with her "infatuating principle" of unnecessary thrift (40) and her keen eye for the main chance, which tends to light on such trifles as cream cheeses, recipes, plants, pheasants' eggs, scraps of green baize and "supernumerary jellies," can be regarded almost as a rather surprising parody of Miss Crawford. Mrs Norris might be understood as using her perquisites as a kind of balm to her perennial discomfort at being the perpetual poor relation. Mary Crawford's envious eye, however, is cast on larger goals – not on such trifles as free meals and carriage rides, but on the impressive fortunes of Mr Rushworth and Tom Bertram (161, 434). And just as Mrs Norris, projecting her own weaknesses, judges others by herself, seeing the Bertrams' trusted workers as "encroaching" (162), warning the meek Fanny against "putting herself forward" (234), so does Mary Crawford.

This comparison may perhaps seem rather far-fetched, however, as it is one of many possible parallels, given that virtually every character in *Mansfield Park* is represented in terms of his or her diseased relationship with money. Tom Bertram is the conventional wastrel heir so often found in eighteenth and nineteenth century-drama and fiction, "with all the liberal dispositions of an eldest son who feels born only for expense and enjoyment" (48). His sense of entitlement so deadens his feelings that he is scarcely affected by the awareness that his extravagance has cost his brother a valuable source of income. Maria too is something of a stock figure in her vanity and acquisitiveness. Both Bertram sisters already show their bent towards materialism in childhood. On Fanny's first day at Mansfield Park "they make her a generous present of some of their least valued toys," and then take up "whatever might be their favourite holiday sport of the moment, making artificial flowers or wasting gold paper" (45). As children, then, they are connected with the artifice and waste that will be so much a part of their adult characters. To use the critical terms of Edward Copeland, Austen represents them as budding consumers.³⁵ Lady Bertram's sense of the inevitable connection between wealth and sexuality is such that she only decides that Fanny is good-looking after her niece is courted by a rich man. And Sir Thomas combines a strong sense of duty with a strong sense of the financially and socially expedient. At Mansfield, only Fanny and Edmund are immune, though even Edmund seems to be attracted by the glamour of wealth. Some of Mary's gifts are natural, but her accomplishments, her self-confidence and her elegance are all the product of considerable wealth. Elsie Michie suggests that Edmund's "simultaneous attraction" to Fanny and Mary "marks the way that in a commercial society wealth may appear so attractive that it will no longer be possible to distinguish it from virtue, the two will look the same" (15).

Even *Lovers' Vows*, the play famously rehearsed but never acted at Mansfield, concerns misguided attitudes towards financial gain and social position. Tellingly, the character who must and finally does correct his beliefs and behaviour in this regard is the patriarch, the parallel of Sir Thomas, Baron Wildenhaim, the father of Amelia and Frederick and the lover of Agatha. He wants to marry Amelia to Count Cassel because of the Count's "Birth and Fortune" (Inchbald 586), even though Amelia, detesting the Count, asserts, "birth and fortune are such old-fashioned things to me, I care nothing about either" (Inchbald 613). Robert Miles comments on the parallel here between the Baron and Sir Thomas: "The Baron's encouragement of Count Cassel reprises Sir Thomas's tolerance of the foolish Rushworth" (Miles 99). In addition, when the baron discovers that his long-discarded mistress, Agatha, bore him a now-adult son, his first reaction is an attempt to buy her off with "a purse of gold" (Inchbald 621), which she rejects angrily. *Lovers' Vows* is a comedy, however, and the Baron at last comes to allow Amelia to marry for love, not money, and himself marries Agatha. The comedy of *Mansfield Park* operates rather differently.

Austen presents a fine display of the various kinds of attitudes towards money at Mansfield Park in a discussion arising from the subject of the improvements at Sotherton: what might have turned into a debate about aesthetics or the obligations of property becomes very much an exposé of different attitudes towards money. Maria, calmly assuming the prenuptial right to spend Rushworth's money, tells him his "best friend" would be the notoriously expensive Humphry Repton. Mrs Norris, who likes to spend anyone's money except her own and to vaunt her rich connections, agrees with her favorite niece, telling Rushworth that he need not worry if Repton's rates were doubled. Edmund, doing his best to gloss over Mr Rushworth's inanities, announces that he would like to oversee his own improvements, while Mary Crawford, who regards beautiful surroundings as a commodity like any other, would gladly pay to avoid the trouble (84). Henry Crawford admits to having been a "devourer" of his own pleasure in improvement and to have finished all the improvements to his property at the age of twenty-one. Fanny, meanwhile, mourns the approaching doom of the avenue at Sotherton and thinks of Cowper, unable as she is even to contemplate the power to choose of a property-owner.

All this characteristic chatter seems harmless enough; but Austen represents the Bertram family's unhappiness and the novel's catastrophes as being occasioned by their false attitudes towards money. Maria's adultery and eventual imprisonment with Mrs Norris are a natural consequence of marrying for money. Sir Thomas's distress is a result of having encouraged this marriage while knowing Maria's motives in marrying Rushworth perfectly well. Mrs Norris suffers acutely without recognizing that she has helped "dearest Mrs Rushworth" into a disastrous match. Rushworth suffers humiliation because he has bought what should not have been for sale: the narrative voice comments, "his punishment followed his conduct, as did a deeper punishment the deeper guilt of his wife" (460).

Austen also represents, though less directly, Henry Crawford's loss of happiness as a result of his attitudes towards his financial life. For Crawford, property implies pleasure rather than responsibility. He has treated his estate at Everingham as merely a source of money, game and the pleasures of "Improvement," until he is prompted to consider changing his ways by his understanding of Fanny's values. At Portsmouth it is clear that he has learnt that Fanny's attitude towards money is quite different from his own or his sister's and that he can ingratiate himself with her by presenting himself as "the friend of the poor and the oppressed" on his own property (406). Yet instead of returning straightway to these obligations he is tempted to resume his power over Maria: "had he done as he intended, and as he knew he ought, by going down to Everingham after his return from Portsmouth, he might have been deciding his own happy destiny," and have ended up happily married to Fanny (462). His decision to choose immediate pleasure in the exercise of sexual power rather than his responsibilities as a landowner results in his loss of "his best, most estimable and endeared acquaintance," as well as "the woman whom he had rationally, as well as passionately loved" (464).

Apart from Edmund Bertram, the only characters Austen represents as being free from venality are the younger Prices. In a novel, that is, in which, as John Wiltshire says, nearly every character is extremely wealthy (*Cambridge Companion* 59), it is the few characters who know something of poverty who see money as connected with work and social responsibility rather than with sex, luxury, influence and indulgence. And if Edmund is exceptional among the Bertrams, it is partly because he has always known he will have to support himself by professional work.[36] However, Austen's representation of the Prices' house in Portsmouth, with its grubbiness, incessant noise, lack of consideration for others, poor food and confined spaces indicates that she has no intention of romanticizing poverty. Perhaps the contrast between rich and poor in *Mansfield Park* argues that Austen would see some truth in the assertion made by a (very rich) character in one of Iris Murdoch's novels: "'it is only poor people who don't want money, they lack the concept'" (*Nuns and Soldiers* 483). Austen, of course, accounts for it differently. The young Prices have some rather uncomfortable privileges: "the advantages of early hardship and discipline, and the consciousness of being born to struggle and endure" (468).

To return in closing to the West Indies: I have argued that Sir Thomas's position as owner of an Antiguan property relates to one of the novel's ongoing ethical concerns, which is the damage done by false attitudes towards money and by the failure to question societal norms in regard to money.[37] I might be regarded as being engaged in what John Wiltshire calls "decolonizing" the novel, in that my attention is directed firmly, as Said says Austen's is, towards England, towards English relationships and English failures. Sir Thomas's position as an Antiguan landowner is symptomatic of his attitudes towards the acquisition and retention of wealth. However, Robert Irvine makes a valid claim: "*Mansfield Park* provides us with a way of thinking about the interpenetration of global economic relations with everyday life. A postcolonial approach to this text could remind us of our ongoing implication in those relations" (140). Reading *Mansfield Park* can not only remind us of our implication in these relations but also direct our attention towards the habitual cupidity on which such relations are based.

The word "principle" is most often associated in this novel with two characters, Sir Thomas and Fanny Price. Sir Thomas at the end of the novel is "sick of ambition and mercenary connections, prizing more and more the sterling good of principle and temper" (466). He has discovered what the reader has known since the first page, which is that his principles have been compromised by his materialism. Fanny Price, who is so lacking in natural cupidity that, even when playing cards, it is necessary for another person to "sharpen her avarice" (252), consistently refuses compromises based on material advantage. She is perhaps the character who has the most to gain from such compromises, given her poverty and her marginal status; but perhaps these disadvantages in themselves make her less open to such temptations. If she is Sir Thomas's moral heir, it is through adhering to his principles in a way that he found impossible himself.

Chapter Five

SPEECH AND SILENCE IN *EMMA*

From its title-page – *Emma: A Novel* – and its first two words – "Emma Woodhouse" – on, Jane Austen's most perfect narrative focuses on one woman, confining itself almost entirely to Emma's own consciousness.[1] Yet Austen's concern here is not with the individual consciousness in isolation but with the individual in the family as well as the larger community. Book I focuses on Emma in Hartfield, while the later books concern Emma both in Hartfield and in Highbury.[2] As Jan Fergus writes, in *Emma*, "Highbury as a community takes centre stage" (*Jane Austen* 152). And the little town is imagined as closely and lovingly as any of its inhabitants, and perhaps plays as important a role in the novel.[3]

In any small close-knit community such as Highbury, with its obligations, benefits and irritations, speech – communication – is central.[4] Accordingly, *Emma*, more than any other of Austen's novels, emphasizes the significance of speech, not only through its brilliant dialogue, but also through an intense consciousness of speech habits and their implications.[5] All Austen's novels show a sensitivity to idiolects. J. F. Burrows' studies confirm that "the evidence of stable *differentiation* between character and character, idiolect and idiolect, is far more pronounced than the evidence of *variation* within any one idiolect" (39).[6] In *Emma*, this differentiation is especially striking, and this novel's characters and narrative voice alike pay more conscious attention to its implications.[7] Miss Bates, Mr Elton, Mrs Elton, Harriet, Mr Woodhouse – all are recognizable every time they open their mouths, not just because of the content of their speeches but also because of the characteristic ways in which they express themselves – their various idiolects.[8] These idiolects certainly reflect education, gender and social class, but they also communicate the peculiar viewpoint of each character.[9] As well as being in part defined and expressed by their own speech habits, characters comment extensively on each other's diction and locutions and discuss the implications of language use, which is also the subject of narrative comment. As Juliet McMaster says, "the discriminating members of Highbury society have a virtually professional expertise in each others' language" ("Secret Language" 121).

The first chapter of the novel establishes immediately the various needs different people have in conversation – the need for comfort, for stimulus, for play, for exchange of information – as well as the different ways of understanding and managing conversation. The narrative is triggered by Miss Taylor's marriage to Mr Weston, and Emma is well aware that the new Mrs Weston's move to Randalls, involving the loss of a companion "to whom [Emma] can speak every thought as it arose," leaves Emma in danger of "intellectual solitude" (56). Emma's conversational needs cannot be met at home as her father is not her intellectual equal and cannot supply the kind of "conversation, either rational or playful" that she needs (56).[10] Emma, however, can supply her father with the constant "chat" required to soothe and distract him. Like Elizabeth Bennet, Emma must negotiate daily life with an unintelligent parent, but while in Elizabeth's case, a minimal courtesy towards her mother is all that is either given or required, Mr Woodhouse demands – and gets – from Emma a more active consideration.

As soon as this strong contrast between father and daughter in terms of conversational needs is established, Austen introduces Mr Knightley. Once he arrives, we see how skilfully Emma has learnt to adapt her conversation to suit her company. Her mode of speech to Mr Knightley (whose own tendency to dogmatism is also apparent in this opening scene) is completely different from her mode of speech to her father. Burrows observes: "Emma's sub-idiolects are more sharply differentiated [than Elizabeth Bennet's]. Her condescension, affectionate as it is, towards her father, is suitably registered and easily understood" (187). She speaks to Mr Woodhouse as one does to a fractious child, gently coaxing and persuading: "'Not a tear, and hardly a long face to be seen. Oh! no, we all felt that we were going to be only half a mile apart, and were sure of meeting every day,'" she says, cajoling her father into cheerfulness over the wedding of "'poor Miss Taylor'" (59). She has taken on early – too early – the role of daughter-as-parent, which may well have made her less ready to treat other people as equals. With Mr Knightley she is free to be serious, playful or argumentative as she wishes. Austen also immediately presents the linguistic contrast between a doting father who cannot imagine his daughter "not being thought perfect by every one" and Mr Knightley, who "never flatters" (59), though he will eventually come to find Emma "faultless in spite of all her faults" (368). Largely through speech then the first chapter of *Emma* both sets up the novel's problem and indicates a solution for it, a solution worked out in the body of the novel.

In *Emma*, Austen gently but invariably moralizes speech acts. Anthony Mandal comments that, throughout Austen's novels, "the use of an inadequate vocabulary points to an inattentiveness to the ethical boundaries that circumscribe human action" (25). In this novel above all, "death and life are in the power of the tongue," to quote the biblical Book of Proverbs (18:21).

Allusions to Death, Life, and the Bible may sound rather overstrained in reference to Austen's comedy, in which, after all, nothing of any great external significance happens. Its earliest critic, Walter Scott, pointed out that "*Emma* has even less story than either [*Sense and Sensibility* or *Pride and Prejudice*]" (419).[11] Any catastrophe that threatens is averted. Mrs Weston's poultry houses are raided, so Emma and Mr Knightley can be happy. Mrs Churchill conveniently dies, so Frank and Jane can be happy. Robert Martin's renewed proposal rapidly cures Harriet's broken heart. Yet the seriousness of this comedy is beyond dispute: there is a strong sense throughout of the communal obligation of averting other people's pain and furthering other people's well-being.

The novel's insistence on the community indicates its ethical concerns. As Tobin Siebers says, "at the heart of ethics resides the overriding human desire to live in community with other people and no ethical concept exists for long that does not ultimately work to satisfy this interest" (13). All Austen's novels show cruelty – the small cruelties that families and other social groups constantly inflict on each other – "with such imaginative cogency as necessarily to recommend kindness," as Christopher Ricks indicates (101). This novel, however, emphasizes the need for kindness more intensely because of its stress on community both within and beyond the family, as well as its representations of the various vulnerabilities of members of the community, such as Harriet Smith, Jane Fairfax, Miss Bates and Mr Woodhouse. Mr Woodhouse plays an important role in Emma's education simply through his deficiencies. From an early age she has had to learn to live with a man who lacks both energy and common sense. Living in a community is not necessarily a matter of living with one's peers, intellectual or otherwise. Just as in *Sense and Sensibility*, where Marianne Dashwood has to learn to coexist with Mrs Jennings and the Middletons, Emma has to learn to live with the undiscriminating Mr Weston, the vulgar Eltons, the garrulous Miss Bates. They are part of her community and so she owes them charity and consideration. It is not by chance that this is the only one of the six novels in which the heroine is seen in that most characteristic activity of the nineteenth-century lady, charitable visits to the poor.[12] Of course, some of this obligation towards others takes the very concrete form of a "whole hind quarter" of pork, a sack of apples or a pitcher of broth (178, 119, 226).[13] Most often, though, social obligation works through the spoken word.

* * *

Every character, except perhaps Miss Bates, inevitably fails in this obligation of charity from time to time, most notably Emma herself. At home, with her father or her sister's family, Emma is kindness itself. Like Darcy, whose manners in Hertfordshire are so different from his manners at Pemberley, it is when Emma moves beyond her own family circle, from Hartfield into Highbury, that she is occasionally tempted into malice. And Emma's worst misdeeds, her worst offences against the community, are verbal. Indeed, it is arguable that, at this period, the moral life of gentry women – "ladies" – most often involved speech rather than action, because it was through speech that they were able to exercise a degree of freedom. The most memorable of Emma's offences – one that she herself will soon recognize as "so brutal, so cruel" (326) – is her unkindness to Miss Bates at Box Hill, when she cannot resist a jibe at the older woman's speech habits as sure to lead her to exceed the limit of "three things very dull indeed" (322). If we wince at this small incident it is because Austen puts us in Emma's place, so well do we understand both Emma's original temptation and her later contrition: Miss Bates is clearly infuriating and clearly good-nature itself. In addition, as Pamela Bromberg comments, Emma's mockery "imperils the basic values of caretaking and concern that underlie community" (132).[14] Moreover, Austen perhaps flatters her readers into believing that they share the temptations of a wit, such as Emma, to make amusing if hurtful remarks.[15]

The dangers of wit – and especially female wit – were a commonplace of the period. Fordyce's *Sermons for Young Women*, so tedious to Lydia Bennet, warns that "men of the best sense have usually been averse to the thought of marrying a witty female" (1.90). Hannah More describes wit as "the most captivating but the most dreaded of all talents: most dangerous to those who have it, most feared by those who have it not [...] A woman who possesses this quality has received a most dangerous present, perhaps not less so than beauty itself" (*Letters to Young Ladies* 32–3), while the well-known conduct writer, Dr Gregory, comments that "wit is so flattering to vanity, that those who possess it become intoxicated, and lose all self-command" (30).[16] Well, yes – especially when it is a very hot day and everyone in the company is feeling rather irritable. However, though Miss Bates is hurt, she soon forgives Emma. The ill-effects of Emma's other verbal misdeeds last longer. Emma's failure in "the duty of woman by woman" (221) in imparting to Frank Churchill her "abominable suspicions" about Jane Fairfax and Mr Dixon is indeed, as she comes to realize, "unpardonable" in itself (359). It also causes embarrassment to Emma herself as well as to Jane. Again, Emma's heedless fostering of Harriet's infatuation with Mr Elton, "talk[ing] her" into love (154), as she talked her out of love with Robert Martin, gives Harriet five months of unnecessary misery. The far fewer words of encouragement she gives Harriet in relation to her second love (or perhaps, Harriet being Harriet, her third love) backfire, of course, causing both Emma and Harriet brief but acute pain.

Other characters, of course, also commit significant verbal aggressions, to adopt Juliet McMaster's phrase (*Talk* 73). Frank Churchill's characteristic teasing of Jane about a tune that was "danced at Weymouth" (229) may indeed be "not kind," as Elizabeth Newark says (215), but his words at Box Hill, which Jane knows only too well how to interpret, are far more cruel: "'How many a man has committed himself on a short acquaintance, and rued it all the rest of his life!'" he says, angrily and pointedly (324). John Knightley is ill-tempered, George Knightley scolds – or at least, he scolds Emma, reducing her to tears. But like Emma, these characters acknowledge and sometimes even feel shame for their verbal affronts. They are sensitive and intelligent enough to understand what they have done.

But those who offend most through their words are quite incapable of perceiving their offences and are therefore incapable of change. Consider Mrs Elton: Augusta Hawkins Elton's use of language resembles that of advertising rather than of literature or conversation. She uses language not so much for communication and interaction as for the greater glory of Augusta Hawkins Elton. Virtually every speech of Mrs Elton's boasts – of her liveliness, her "resources," her servants, her clothes, her good taste, her husband's importance in the community, her brother-in-law's wealth, his rich friends, his barouche-landau. She manages to inflict many wounds in the process of self-aggrandizement. At the dinner party at Hartfield, for instance, she bullies Jane Fairfax incessantly, first about her visits to the post office, and then about getting a position as governess as soon as possible. She refuses to listen to Jane's firm but quiet protests, speaking in terms of "'exert[ing] authority'" over Jane (266).[17] Such self-aggrandizing patronage allows her to advertise her belief in her power and general superiority, as well as the fact that she has more than one manservant (to collect Jane's letters) and sundry rich connections (to employ Jane as governess).[18] The implications of this episode are underlined by its ending – by the brilliant comedy of the dialogue, or rather the dual monologue, between her and Mr Weston, in which Mr Weston wishes only to talk about his son and Mrs Elton wishes only to talk about Mrs Elton. Marilyn Butler asserts that "none of the comic characters communicate. They surround themselves with a web of words but with words that convey their own selfhood, their individuality and make little or no impact on the consciousness of others" (271).[19] More accurately, perhaps, the consciousness of others makes little or no impact on these speakers. They are incapable of proper attention. That is as true of Mr Weston as of Mrs Elton, but, as with Miss Bates's verbosity and Mr Woodhouse's inanity, his verbal offences are easily forgiven because of his patent good nature and because he is obsessed not with himself but with his son.

Mrs Elton's speech is the subject of frequent comment by the other characters, both for its content and its manner. Emma notes especially Mrs Elton's pretentious ways of speaking of other people, which show not only her wish for self-aggrandizement, but also her ignorance of polite usage as well as of grammatical Italian. After her first tête-à-tête with Mrs Elton, Emma exclaims to herself, "Knightley! – I could not have believed it. Knightley! – never seen him in her life before, and call him Knightley! [...] her Mr E, and her cara sposo" (255). Chapman's edition corrects Mrs Elton's mistake and prints "caro sposo," but it seems significant that she gets it wrong twice – and that Emma seems to observe this.[20] Emma's distaste at this point may be based largely on class prejudice. Mrs E. is non-U.[21] Yet her solecisms are offensive, because they show both presumption (in addressing a new acquaintance as if he were an intimate) and affectation (in unnecessary use of a foreign language).

Her husband's speech habits – apart from his perpetual and meaningless "exactly so" – have perhaps a more unpleasant significance. Both the Knightley brothers observe the great difference between Mr Elton's speech with women and with men. Mr Knightley warns Emma, "'Elton may talk sentimentally but he will act rationally [...] from his general way of talking in unreserved moments, when there are only men present, I am convinced that he does not mean to throw himself away'" (101). The less tolerant John Knightley comments, "'I never in my life saw a man more intent on being agreeable than Mr Elton. It is downright labour to him where ladies are concerned. With men he can be rational and unaffected, but when he has ladies to please, every feature works'" (136). With women, Elton is a hypocrite. Austen represents him as a reasonably responsible clergyman, active enough in his parish, talking to his poor parishioners about parish relief and conferring with the more prosperous parishioners, magistrates, overseers and churchwardens, about parish affairs. Professionally he is apparently competent, but socially – with women – he is merely self-seeking. While Emma thinks that he is Harriet's suitor, she notes his excessive gallantry merely with amusement, observing his care "that nothing ungallant, nothing that did not breathe a compliment to the sex, should pass his lips" (104). She notes, "there was a sort of parade in his speeches which was very apt to incline her to laugh. She ran away to indulge the inclination" (115).

The truth about the hypocrisy inherent in his gallantry does begin to dawn on her at one point, when she thinks, "this man is almost too gallant to be in love" (88); she quickly brushes the realization aside, however. Emma is, typically if regrettably, more sensitive to what offends Emma than to what might offend Emma's dear friend. It is not until Emma is forced to recognize that she herself is his object, that she recognizes Elton's falsifications for what they are: "There had been no real affection either in his language or manners. Sighs and fine words had been given in abundance; but she could hardly devise any set of expressions or fancy any tone of voice less allied with real love" (153). Such falsity is insulting. "Person counts for little, it is plain, in Mr Elton's quest for a wife," Peter Knox-Shaw comments, writing of Elton's rapid transfer of his attentions – "within a month!" – from Emma to Miss Hawkins (209). Elton's "sighs and fine words" are addressed not to Harriet Smith or to Emma Woodhouse, but to Emma's £30, 000.

Through Emma's gradual recognition of Mr Elton's character, Austen represents gallantry with the same distaste shown by Mary Wollstonecraft in *A Vindication of the Rights of Woman*. Wollstonecraft writes of "the cold unmeaning intercourse of gallantry" (221) and exclaims "what can be more disgusting than the impudent dross of gallantry" (256). Wollstonecraft's concern is the way that gallantry persistently sexualizes women, rather than humanizing them: gallantry is "impudent dross," "cold" and "unmeaning," because it does not allow for the possibility of rational interchange between men and women. In *Emma*, Austen seems as sensitive to the inherent insincerity and falsification involved in gallantry as to its denial of rationality.

Such hypocrisy as Elton's is especially offensive in a text such as this, in which truth, like charity, is paramount. Elton, like a coarser Frank Churchill, fails to observe the standards of strict honesty. Emma, when driven to consider "what a man should be," talks about "that strict adherence to truth and principle, that disdain of trick and littleness, which a man should display in every transaction of his life" (342). Plainly, her standards are set by Mr Knightley. Truth in this narrative is related to love, or more precisely to the appropriate male love object, for here the males most worthy to attract females – Mr Knightley, Mr Martin – are the truth-tellers. Mr Knightley indeed stands in sharp contrast to Mr Elton in two crucial ways: he is "'not a gallant man, but he is a very humane one'" (215), as Emma says, unlike the man who cruelly exposes Harriet to ridicule at the ball; and he is invariably honest. Mr Knightley is represented as nothing if not honest. One of his first speeches in the novel is "'Emma knows I never flatter her'" – a pointed contrast with the fine speeches of Mr Elton a little later. In his relation with Emma it is in part "the beauty of truth and sincerity" that Knightley values (377).

Emma shares his values and, after her engagement, is wounded by her need to conceal certain details for Harriet's sake. She finds the need to practice a degree of deceit towards Mr Knightley "little inferior to the pain of having made Harriet unhappy" (390). And, when Harriet is safely in the hands of Mr Martin and the need for reticence is over,

> high in rank of [Emma's] most serious and heartfelt felicities, was the reflection that all concealment from Mr Knightley would soon be over. The disguise, equivocation, mystery, so hateful to her to practice might soon be over. She could now look forward to giving him that full and perfect confidence which her disposition was most ready to welcome as a duty. (399)

For Emma, sincerity is a value she accepts both instinctively and intellectually. She cannot have the same degree of honesty with a father she always needs to tend and to manipulate as she can with Mr Knightley. Moreover her father's own speech is in certain ways closer to Mr Elton's than to Mr Knightley's; he enjoys the flatteries of Elton's pretentious charade because, as his daughter says, "'he loves anything that pays a woman a compliment. He has the tenderest spirit of gallantry towards us all'" (110). Mr Woodhouse's gallantry, however, is based on courtesy as well as mindless convention, and is an aspect of his dislike of change. It is not directly manipulative, as are the compliments of Mr Elton and Frank Churchill, being directed at other people's comfort rather than his own ends.

Elton's speech, with its compliments and "parade," offends against sincerity. It also offends against the values implicit in *Emma* in a less serious but related way. "'One man's style must not be the rule of another's,'" says Mr Knightley, as he reads Frank Churchill's letter, having finally achieved a degree of tolerance for Frank (376). All the same, it is quite clear that he does take his own style as a rule and that his style is, like his author's, the plain style, quite at odds with the "fine complimentary" approach of Frank Churchill and Mr Elton (376) – or even the scrupulous politeness of Mr Woodhouse. The treatment of the plain style in *Emma* implies that it is an indication of moral and intellectual quality as well as of good taste, that it is of value to the community in general, not merely an indication of social class. When Knightley asks Emma to marry him, he uses what the narrative voice describes as "plain, unaffected, gentleman-like English" (379), a significant conjunction of adjectives, placing the moral ("plain" and "unaffected," which imply "truthful") alongside the social ("gentleman-like"). Knightley himself seems to think of his own plain-spokenness as a guarantee of sincerity: "'I cannot make speeches,'" he tells Emma, "'If I loved you less I might be able to talk about it more. But you know what I am. – You hear nothing but truth from me'"(366). The narrative voice seems to support this implied connection between plain speech and sincerity. When the Knightley brothers meet, for instance: "'How d'ye do, George?' and 'John, how are you?' succeeded in the true English style, burying under a calmness that seemed all but indifference, the real attachment which would have led either of them, if requisite, to do almost anything for the good of the other" (127). Knightley's bluntness occasionally verges on rudeness, but never quite crosses the line. Margaret Kirkham believes he is insulting to Miss Bates, as offensive as Emma at Box Hill, in asking her, "'Are you mad to let your niece sing herself hoarse in this manner?'" (*E* 220, Kirkham 133). Miss Bates, however, clearly recognizes his good intentions and minds no more than Emma minds when he affectionately calls her a "'nonsensical girl'" (208).

Use of the plain style also indicates Robert Martin's fine qualities. His language use is described in precisely the same terms as that of Mr Knightley. Emma is snobbishly surprised by the style of his letter to Harriet, proposing marriage: "There were not merely no grammatical errors, but as a composition *it would not have disgraced a gentleman*; the language, though *plain*, was strong and *unaffected*, and the sentiments it conveyed very much to the credit of the writer. It was short, but expressed good sense, warm attachment, liberality, propriety, even delicacy of feeling" (89 – my emphases). Mr Knightley, too, praises Robert Martin for his use of plain language: "'I never hear better sense from anyone than from Robert Martin. He always speaks to the purpose; open, straight forward and very well judging'" (96). Like his landlord's, Robert Martin's language communicates warmth, openness and sincerity. In *Emma*, verbal style indicates moral style.

***

The title of this chapter alludes to silence as well as speech, and silences are essential to this novel, which would have virtually no plot without them. Many people, notably P. D. James, who knows about these things, have written about *Emma* in terms of the detective story or mystery, and such narratives demand silences, gaps in the available information. They face the novelist with "the twin problems of suppression and disclosure," to use Nancy Armstrong's phrase (145). But silences in *Emma* work beyond the level of plot. Like speech, silences – failures or refusals to communicate, feelings that are beyond words[22] – can be aggressions against the communal values on which Highbury depends. Even those silences that Alison Sulloway regards as characteristic of women and "their millennia long silences, half-silences, denials and evasions" (161) can be used aggressively. Jane's silence, and even more so Frank's combinations of silence and misleading speech, offend in that they unsettle normal community interactions in a close-knit society, a society in which people are accustomed to expect to understand the network of relationships amongst which they live. Significantly, neither Frank nor Jane is properly a member of the community, both having been brought up elsewhere. For Emma, born and bred in Highbury, Frank's concealment of his engagement to Jane is an abuse of those communal values. She attacks Frank's behaviour, and her implicit grounds are again the importance of those standards embodied in Mr Knightley – the obligation of truth and sincerity in a community. When Mrs Weston tells Emma about the secret engagement between Frank and Jane, Emma, outraged, asks:

"What has it been but a system of hypocrisy and deceit, – espionage and treachery? – To come among us with professions of openness and simplicity; and such a league in secret to judge us all! – Here we have been, the whole winter and spring, completely duped, fancying ourselves all on an equal footing of truth and honour." (344)

Emma's anger, of course, arises partly from her embarrassment at her own foolishness in talking to Frank about Jane and Mr Dixon. But she is right in her judgment of Frank, too, in that, though he is intelligent, good-natured and well-bred enough to avoid the worst offences of the Eltons, his value for truth and direct dealing is suspect, to say the least. "'I am the wretchedest being in the world for a civil falsehood,'" Frank says; but even as he speaks, he is deceiving Emma about his knowledge of the origin of Jane's piano, and he can find plenty of other ways to distort the truth, both through speech and through silence (223).

While silences can be abused, in almost any society they are sometimes desirable and inevitable: "seldom, very seldom does complete truth belong to any human disclosure," says the narrative voice. Moral obligations are complex. Emma may love "every thing that is decided and open" (388) and acknowledge the beauty of frankness, but she cannot tell the whole truth about her recent emotional history to Mr Knightley without wounding Harriet further than she has been wounded already. Her behaviour implicitly recognizes her conflicting obligations to Harriet and to Mr Knightley. The paramount moral values of this novel, truth and charity, are occasionally and realistically incompatible, as they are in *Sense and Sensibility*: as Elinor Dashwood knows to her cost, there are occasions for "telling lies when politeness requires it" (*S&S* 149–50). Truth sometimes has the potential for damage. *Emma*, with its stress on community, puts forward the ideal of a careful, complex and intelligent negotiation between speech and silence, between openness and tact, for the benefit of communal living.

Indeed, although Emma undoubtedly has the "open temper" that Mr Knightley loves (262), she is also a mistress of the kindly or polite silence.[23] She has had plenty of exercise in the art from dealing with her father. As Claudia Johnson says, "Emma has ready stores of 'politeness,' which enable her to respect what is delicate by leaving it unsaid" (*Jane Austen* 129). In relation to these silences, Johnson also comments on Emma's verbal cruelties:

> Shameful as these infractions are, they stand out precisely because they are so infrequent, and if Mrs Elton's presence on the scene helps us to identify and deplore them, it also helps appreciate how much better Emma handles herself by comparison. (*Jane Austen* 130)

Emma, unlike Mrs Elton, sees the necessity of negotiating between the values of truth and those of charity, sometimes through speech and sometimes through her own silence. When she has to listen to John Knightley's complaints about Mr Weston's unwanted hospitality, for instance, "she had resolution enough to refrain from making any answer at all. She could not be complying, she dreaded being quarrelsome; her heroism reached only to silence" (137). The comfort of family relations, perhaps especially among relations-in-law, depends on such restraint.[24] It is necessarily an intelligent negotiation, and Mr Woodhouse is incapable of perceiving the necessity for the kind of silences that would prevent him from irritating his son-in-law, just as the irritable John Knightley is incapable of the kind of consistent self-control that would prevent him from voicing that irritation. Similarly, when Mr Weston, who is virtually a family member through his marriage to Miss Taylor, is justifying himself for tactlessly drawing the Eltons into the Box Hill expedition, "Emma denied none of it aloud, and agreed to none of it in private" (309). A similar note is struck in *Sanditon*, when Charlotte Heywoood, disgusted at Lady Denham's meanness, "kept her countenance and she kept a civil silence. She could not carry her forbearance farther" (181). Again, Emma keeps her engagement from her father for some weeks in order to save him – and perhaps herself – from extra anxiety during Mrs Weston's confinement. In *Emma*, silences are justified if they are based on a concern for communal comfort rather than on self-interest.

Sometimes, inevitably, Emma's silence arises from self-protection rather than politeness or consideration for others: when she realizes that Harriet loves Mr Knightley, she keeps defensively silent about her own feelings, but what she says to Harriet is no more than the truth: "'Harriet, I will only venture to declare, that Mr Knightley is the last man in the world, who would intentionally give any woman the idea of his feeling for her more than he really does'" (352). As André Brink points out, "in a situation where open revolt or defiance is ruled out, one of the only possible alternatives to compliance is silence, and on occasion Emma does resort to it" (304). Compliance might involve hypocrisy; revolt might be destructive; silence preserves both the moral and the social order.

This sense of the need to negotiate between speech and silence for the sake of the group is something Emma shares with Mr Knightley, for of all the many couples in this marriage comedy, they are the only pair held together by shared principles. Austen demonstrates the fundamental agreement between Knightley and Emma by showing them working together for the comfort of the family group – by organizing speech and silence. At this point Austen indicates that their marriage will be based on the ethical as well as the erotic. Throughout the visit of John and Isabella Knightley to Highbury Emma and Mr Knightley cooperate to negotiate peace in the family circle, both at Hartfield and at Randalls, by providing speech as a diversion so as to protect the necessary silences about certain sensitive subjects – rival doctors, seaside holidays: "At times, almost inadvertently," says Mary Waldron,

> they achieve a kind of instinctual harmony of purpose which hints at a latent kindredship of spirit – as for instance during the incipient quarrel between John Knightley and Mr Woodhouse during the family visit to Hartfield, when they both make strenuous and concerted efforts to change the subject [...] and at the snowy Christmas Eve party at Randalls when both combine to extricate Mr Woodhouse. (120)

The closeness and mutual understanding between Emma and Mr Knightley is very clear in the sheer brevity of their exchange about leaving Randalls:

> While the others were variously urging and recommending, Mr Knightley and Emma settled it in a few brief sentences: thus –
> "Your father will not be easy; why do not you go?"
> "I am ready, if the others are."
> "Shall I ring the bell?"
> "Yes, do." (148)

As Juliet McMaster observes, this scene shows them as "essentially compatible partners" ("Secret Language" 129).[25] More than this, it shows obliquely the effective moral and social basis of their relationship.

With Mr Knightley, Emma speaks as an equal, ready to be playful or argumentative as the fancy takes her. Their relationship is at the heart of the novel not just because the novel is a love story, but also because, at its best, that relationship shows the full use of speech as right communication both between two people and, beyond that, between those two people and the family group, then further beyond that to a larger society. In fact, love in *Emma* is presented in terms of such communication.[26] As Butler suggests, Emma and Mr Knightley are both "supreme in dialogue" (272). Their unique relationship shows itself most clearly in their conversation, as does that of Darcy and Elizabeth. The dialogues between Knightley and Emma are perhaps the product of a more mature and complex art, or a more mature and complex ethical vision. Darcy and Elizabeth fence, while Knightley and Emma are represented as both fighting together and working together. Their dialogues show the two lovers acting together within a community, and, in part, for the sake of that community.[27] James Boyd White aptly observes that Austen is

> interested not only in the way the individual reconstitutes his language and in those relationships between two persons in which education can

proceed – between Emma and Mr Knightley in the world of the novel, and between Austen and her reader in the text itself—but in the relation between the social worlds thus established and the larger world: that of the family, the village and perhaps, by implication, England itself. (163)

* * *

Emma begins this novel dependent for her everyday conversation on her father, conversation that must always be predicated on her intellectual superiority and her skill in managing him. At the end of the novel she will share her everyday conversation with Knightley, with whom she can converse as an equal. Mr Woodhouse, as a "kind-hearted polite old man," causes comparatively little pain, but the combination of his lack of intellect and the privileged position that facilitates his "habits of gentle selfishness" have left him without the capacity to imagine that "other people could feel differently from himself" (57).[28] Inevitably in his talk he fails in attention to others. And so he inadvertently "attack[s]" Emma's peace with his repeatedly voiced regrets about the absence of Miss Taylor or his discomfort on a rainy evening and he irritates John Knightley into the occasional "rational remonstrance" or "sharp retort" (123). He is incapable of change, because of his social position, which puts him beyond criticism, because of his lack of perception and because of habits that are increasingly entrenched with age. Emma equally fails in attention, not, like him, because of a want of wit and energy but because of a surplus of both. She is carried away by her imagination or her tongue and forgets to observe other people's feelings. But her youth, energy and intelligence enable her to change – or at least to come to a position of self-knowledge that is the basis of change.

* * *

It would seem strange to end a chapter on speech in *Emma* without some discussion of Miss Bates, who is indeed "rather a talker," and whose conversation (if one can call it that) is so important for the direction of the narrative. The interactions of Emma and Knightley are directed in part by communal needs. In the community of Highbury Miss Bates is central, both geographically, in her rooms in the house opposite Ford's the haberdashers, and figuratively, in a dozen different ways. Julia Prewitt Brown, indeed, thinks of her as functioning as "a symbol of Highbury itself" (*Approaches* 18). Miss Bates is central – or symbolic – in part because, in a novel so concerned with community obligations, she is both a generous giver and a grateful receiver. She not only fulfils her own obligations, caring for her mother, her niece and her poor neighbours, but also accepts people's charity – both their hindquarters of pork and their kind words. Both her charity and her gratitude, her giving and her receiving, indicate her happy acceptance of her role as a member of a community.

Through Miss Bates, Austen provides a remarkable example of a character who, though she has "no intellectual superiority" (67), unlike Emma and Mr Knightley, nevertheless combines the values of the novel in herself. She is instinctively charitable: "she loved every body, was interested in every body's happiness, quick-sighted to every body's merits" (67);[29] and she is so truthful that even when a social lie is required of her (telling Mr Knightley they have plenty of apples left, explaining Jane's refusal to see Emma), she has to tell the truth (238, 329).[30] She is central in terms of plot, too: most of the clues in this "detective story" depend on Miss Bates's truth-telling. And for the reader, her unceasing speech creates a sense of the wider community beyond the gentry who are the main characters: "Old John Abdy," once the parish clerk, and his son the ostler, the baker's family, the baker's boy, the servants at Hartfield and Donwell as well as her own Patty, "and all the Mistresses and Misses of Highbury" (166) – we are conscious of all these lives going on because Miss Bates tells us about them; she names them for us. Peter Knox-Shaw describes accurately the importance of this setting to the novel: "to an extent that is unique in Austen's fiction the central characters in *Emma* are continually and extensively represented in relation to the many lives that make up the existence of their parish, and the focus on Highbury is never allowed to stray to another setting" (204). It is largely because of Miss Bates's talk that we have such a strong sense of the community of Highbury and its various inhabitants at all social levels. This sense was perhaps best expressed one hundred and thirty-odd years ago by the distinguished Victorian novelist Margaret Oliphant: "It is impossible to conceive a more perfect piece of village geography, a scene more absolutely real […] We know it as well as if we had lived there all our lives and visited Miss Bates every other day" (224).

Chapter Six

DANDIES AND BEAUTIES: THE ISSUE OF GOOD LOOKS IN *PERSUASION*

By the end of *Mansfield Park* Fanny Price has formed a strong mutual attachment with Sir Thomas Bertram and after her marriage they continue to seek each other's company. The possibility of leaving her father to marry Mr Knightley greatly distresses Emma and eventually she and her husband make their home with Mr Woodhouse. Anne Elliot's relationship with her father is very different: any grief she feels over her marriage to Captain Wentworth, a marriage that could take her right away from her family, results from her knowledge that she has "no relations to bestow on him which a man of sense could value" (257). She offers her father the conventional courtesy and external respect required of a dependent daughter by custom and the fifth commandment without feeling obliged to respond to his wishes or share his values. Christine Gibbs says of Anne,

> her mind and opinions are all her own, and when she quietly ignores her father's disapproval of her visits to her impoverished school friend Mrs Smith, Jane Austen makes it clear that the disobedience is morally justified and that it is Sir Walter whose morals are unsound. (49)

She is "ashamed" at his toadying to Lady Dalrymple and finds the heartless elegance of her father and sister "mortifying" (120). Her idea of good company – "clever, well-informed people who have a great deal of conversation" (171) – is remote from Sir Walter's concern with social rank and physical appearance. This contrast between father and daughter in relation to physical appearance is the subject of this chapter, for through this contrast Austen embodies the crucial difference in their consciousness of the external world – not only the human world but also the natural world and the world of ideas. Anne's moral supremacy within the novel is established partly through the manifest inferiority of her own father and that inferiority manifests itself most often through his regard for appearances.

* * *

This examination of differing attitudes to personal appearance begins with a single word – the word "bloom." The first time I read *Persuasion*, as a most *un*-blooming fifteen-year-old, I was struck with and slightly perplexed by the novel's insistence on this word, which I had never before met in quite the sense in which Austen uses it here. Anne Elliot's bloom "vanished early" (6); the passage of time "destroyed her youth and bloom" (61); she had "every beauty excepting bloom" (153). In her book entitled *Bloom* Amy King explores the idea of bloom and the woman-as-flower as it is applied to marriageable young women in nineteenth-century fiction, basing her discussion on the post-Linnaean sexualization of botany. "The marriage plot's focus on the marriageable or blooming girl," she writes of the nineteenth-century novel, "is like Linnaean botany's focus on the flower's bloom" (76). And blooms, both literal and metaphorical, are for pollination.

King discusses *Persuasion*, describing Anne in horticultural terms as "a repeat bloomer" (124), but she writes in more detail of *Pride and Prejudice*, in which both the word and the concept of bloom are less central. She does not comment on the way in which Anne Elliot's fluctuating bloom is represented in the context of an exceptional emphasis throughout the novel on physical beauty, both male and female, as well as on the hazards to beauty and on the absence of beauty.[1] Many readers have flinched at the narrative voice's comments on Mrs Musgrove's "large fat sighings" over her dead son Richard,[2] but this voice should also remind readers that the trivialization of the lives and feelings of the fat, the old or the plain is common enough even in the twenty-first century:

> A large bulky frame has as good a right to be in deep affliction, as the most graceful set of limbs in the world. But, fair or not fair, there are unbecoming conjunctions, which reason will patronize in vain – which taste cannot tolerate, – which ridicule will seize. (101)

Which, if unpalatable, is true of many people in many societies. Sir Walter Elliot, who counts no fewer than eighty-seven plain faces in the streets of Bath one wintry day (163), merely takes to extremes a common human trait. In discussing the novel's repeated concern with personal appearance, I look at early nineteenth-century discourse about both the importance and the interpretation of personal appearances and go on to explore the implications of Austen's insistence on appearances in this novel. The contrast between Sir Walter, who sees people only as faces and bodies, and Anne, who perceives their needs and anxieties, embodies the ethical concerns of this novel.

* * *

There is, obviously, nothing exceptional about a culture's concern with female beauty. From Helen of Troy to the latest issue of *Vogue*, at every period some women have been noted for their personal appearance, for the way their physical attributes mirror both the aesthetic criteria and the related gender and status codes of their society. Jane Austen's England was of course no exception. If such an obvious point needs proving, the first chapter of *Northanger Abbey* provides evidence enough, with its playful assumption that the heroine of a novel, in order to interest a reader, must be "a beauty from her cradle" (41), unlike Catherine Morland.

Most Western cultures at most periods have been rather less concerned with the desirability of male beauty. But during the Regency period in England there was an unusual amount of discourse concerning the physical appearance of males.[3] It was the beginning of the era of the dandy. The *Oxford English Dictionary* records the word "dandy" as coming into vogue in London between 1813 and 1819 as applied to the "'exquisite' or the 'swell' of the period."[4] According to Jerome McGann, the dandy is "one of the few figures which are specifically, that is, historically and thematically, Romantic in character" (3).[5] In the years that produced *Persuasion* – in England the years of high Romanticism, the years of the Regency – Edward Bulwer-Lytton and Alfred D'Orsay were learning their craft and George "Beau" Brummell, the one-time close friend of the future George IV, was in his prime.[6] The celebrity of Beau Brummell, indeed, was such that Lord Byron himself is reported to have said, "I was in favour with Brummell (and that alone was enough to make a man of fashion at that time)" (Medwin 221). The print shops of the period were full of prints and lampoons about dandyism. An anonymous etching of 1817, showing a dandy complete with eyeglass, tailcoat and a collar up to his ears, also records his affected speech: "D-m me if she isn't a Divinity," he remarks of some invisible woman. Another print, this time from 1820, shows a dandy at his dressing table covered with bottles and jars (including Gowland's lotion?). Richard Dighton's engraving, *The Dandy Club* (1818), is crammed with caricatures of gentlemen of varying degrees of ugliness, again all dressed in the high collars and cravats that were de rigueur at the period (Laver 37–9). A contemporary story tells of one Colonel Kelly of the Guards who, when his apartment caught fire, was burnt to death in an effort to save his beautiful boots. As soon as this was known, all the other dandies in town, including Brummell himself, competed hotly for the services of Colonel Kelly's valet – known for his expertise in boot polishing.[7] The Prince Regent himself, unpleasing as he was in his later years – certainly unpleasing to Jane Austen – was notorious for his concern with his appearance.[8] Lord Byron, another of the most visible men of the day, neatly distinguishes himself from the dandies, commenting that he liked them and that "they were always very civil to *me*, though in general they disliked literary people" (Marchand 146 – Byron's emphasis). All the same, Byron shared the dandies' interest in personal appearance, as both his periods of rigorous dieting and the famous 1814 portrait of him in Albanian dress (by Thomas Phillips) testify.[9] The England in which *Persuasion* was written was remarkable in its concern with masculine appearances.

More than any other of Austen's novels, *Persuasion* insists on its setting at a particular time, the autumn and winter of 1814–15. Austen continually reminds her readers about dates and time. As Linda Bree points out, in this novel, "the physical passing of time is constantly marked by numbers […] From the entry in the baronetage on the very first page of the novel […] dates and ages toll in precise measure" (11). Bree reminds us further, "*Persuasion* was the first of Austen's novels to be set firmly at a particular time" (10). The date, as the navy was set ashore with the temporary peace of 1814, is necessary to the plot, but date and setting alike – for Bath is historically associated with the beaux – nudge us into acknowledging that this is a precise social world, the world of the dandy.[10]

Sir Walter Elliot, if not precisely a dandy himself, is obviously at home in such a society.[11] He is, in the words that James Laver uses of Beau Brummell, "a narcissist *pur sang*, a man who loved only himself" (33). As with the dandies, his concern with physical appearance is not directed to the erotic appeal of other people. Sir Walter's gaze persistently rests on versions of himself, in the mirror, in the baronetage, in a distorted form in other human faces. He admires his daughter Elizabeth because she resembles him, both physically and mentally. Indeed, it is on the whole not through any feminine response but rather through Sir Walter's narcissism – "'such a number of looking-glasses'" as Admiral Crofts comments (151) – that Austen represents, as she repeatedly does, the degrees of masculine attraction. It is Sir Walter who speaks with disgust of the "'deplorable looking'" Admiral Baldwin (60) and with moderate approval of the "'fine military figure'" of Colonel Wallis (163), and who is "very much struck" (255) by the good looks of Captain Wentworth.

Sir Walter is an assessor of feminine attractions, too, though they apparently impinge on his self-absorbed consciousness to a lesser extent. Indeed he judges everyone he sees or hears of by his own standards of physical beauty. The late Mrs William Elliot was "a very fine woman" (161), Colonel Wallis is "not an ill-looking man" (161), Mrs Wallis is said to be "an excessively pretty woman, beautiful" (163) – all this in just one brief conversation. The plain and the awkward cannot be tolerated in Sir Walter's domain – unless indeed they happen to be, like the Hon. Miss Carteret, the offspring of a viscount (171). Captain Wentworth becomes acceptable at last not because of his character, his financial position or his naval distinction but merely because of his good looks and "the importance of a man of such an air and appearance as his [...] Captain Wentworth would move about well in [Elizabeth's] drawing-room" (236). As John Wiltshire shows, Sir Walter's society is one in which the male body is as much "an item of social circulation" as the female (*Body* 161).

Significantly, Sir Walter's obsession with personal appearance leads to a strong distaste for and a refusal to accept the traces of the processes of living, the marks of age, weather, grief and experience. Sir Walter sees

> himself and Elizabeth as blooming as ever, amidst the wreck of the good looks of every body else; for he could plainly see how old all the rest of his family and acquaintance were growing. Anne haggard, Mary coarse, every face in the neighbourhood worsting; and the rapid increase of the crow's foot about Lady Russell's temples had long been a distress to him. (49)

His anxiety extends beyond his immediate circle. In a significant passage, Sir Walter speaks of sailors as "'all knocked about and exposed to every climate, and every weather, till they are not fit to be seen. It is a pity they are not knocked on the head at once, before they reach Admiral Baldwin's age [i.e. 40]'" (60). In a novel that ends with a panegyric to "that profession which is, if possible, more distinguished for its domestic virtues than its national importance" (258), Sir Walter's contempt for that profession furthers the sense of him as "a foolish spendthrift baronet" lacking in "principle or sense" (254).

Mrs Clay's response to Sir Walter's outburst, which I quote at length, is telling. She asks Sir Walter:

> "Is not it the same with many other professions, perhaps most other? Soldiers, in active service, are not at all better off: and even in the quieter professions, there is a toil and a labour of the mind, if not of the body, which seldom leaves a man's looks to the natural effect of time. The lawyer plods, quite careworn; the physician is up at all hours, and travelling in all weathers; and even the clergyman [...] is obliged to go into infected rooms, and expose his health and looks to all the injury of a poisonous atmosphere. In fact [...] though every profession is necessary and honourable in its turn, it is only the lot of those who are not obliged to follow any, who can live in a regular way, in the country, choosing

their own hours, following their own pursuits, and living on their own property, without the torment of trying for more; it is only *their* lot, I say, to hold the blessings of health and a good appearance to the utmost: I know no other set of men but what lose some of their personableness when they cease to be quite young." (60–61)

Of course Mrs Clay is indulging in some well-judged flattery of Sir Walter, but Austen is doing more in this passage than merely communicating the intelligent sycophancy of a minor character. Mrs Clay's arguments, like Sir Walter's scorn of the unfortunate Admiral Baldwin, represent the resistance of the Elliot circle to the normal effects on the human body of an active and productive life.

The deviations from the norm of regular beauty that result from time and experience are not to be tolerated. Like the dandies, the Elliot circle sees appearance as a supreme value; much like the unfortunate Colonel Kelly who died for his boots, good looks come before life for them. As John Wiltshire has observed,

> Sir Walter thinks he and his like are immune from time: the narcissistic fantasy of his vanity expresses itself most powerfully in this delusion, which the novel subsequently underscores by emphasizing the changes and vicissitudes wrought by time, and of the human body as an object besieged by its onslaughts. (*Body* 164)

Sir Walter's assumptions are based on an ideal of stasis rather than process, of introversion rather than of extraversion. Sailors professionally must move outwards, in this narrative to the East Indies and the West Indies, while Sir Walter moves to a narrower sphere, from his country estate with its acres and responsibilities to the house at Camden-place – "two walls, perhaps thirty feet asunder" (160). And in this narrative the sailors move outward metaphorically too, extending their sympathies beyond themselves and their families.

The Elliots' assumption that the preservation of personal beauty is a supreme value[12] relates to another form of discourse about appearances current in the late eighteenth and early nineteenth century – the fashionable study of physiognomy. The most famous of the physiognomists during the period was Johann Kaspar Lavater (1741–1801), who published his *Physiognomische Fragmente* in five volumes between 1775 and 1778.[13] The volumes were rapidly translated into French and English and became widely known and discussed, largely because of their many illustrations and popular style. As Stafford et al. have noted, this study "constituted an encyclopaedia of facial flaws" (218).[14] This obsession with tabulating the "incorrect" arises from

Lavater's fundamental assumptions. His views were essentially normalizing and regularizing: deviations from certain proportions and measurements were counted as physical flaws and these physical flaws were seen as correlating with moral and spiritual flaws (Stafford et al. 216).[15] Again, the regularizing, "minimalist" vision of the physiognomists had no sympathy with the changes and excrescences caused by time and experience[16] – not with Anne's haggardness or Mary's coarseness and certainly not with Lady Russell's crows-feet.[17] And Sir Walter might feel some justification for his vanity in the relation Lavater asserts between beauty and moral character (Tytler 70).[18] However, as Wiltshire asserts, "*Persuasion* is a novel which questions on almost every page the tie between beauty or physical vitality and moral goodness" (*Body* 56). Its heroine, like Fanny Price in *Mansfield Park*, has a physical appearance that changes with time and experience and is explicitly in process.

Austen's insistence in *Persuasion* on personal appearance as manifested in the speech and attitudes of Sir Walter and Elizabeth is then in part a response to and a critique of contemporary attitudes towards and anxieties about time and change. The novel comments on a reluctance to accept the natural processes of human life that is common to the leisured and prosperous of all periods, but evinced itself notably in the early nineteenth century, as in the early twenty-first century, in unrealistic attitudes towards the human body.[19] In her portrayal of Sir Walter and Elizabeth, Austen anticipates by fifteen years the metaphors of a less subtle social critic, Thomas Carlyle, who in *Sartor Resartus* (1833) divides England between the dandies and the drudges. As James Eli Adams points out, in Carlyle's diatribe, "the dandy becomes the grotesque icon of an outworn aristocratic order, a figure of self-absorbed, parasitic existence" (21) – a self-absorbed parasitic existence such as that of Sir Walter Elliot. Virginia Woolf suggests that in *Persuasion* "there is an asperity in her comedy which suggests that she has almost ceased to be amused by the vanities of a Sir Walter […] The satire is harsh and the comedy crude" (143). Similarly Margaret Kirkham comments that "Sir Walter Elliot is treated more harshly than any other Austen Patriarch" (149). This asperity, this lack of sympathy, surely reflects the fact that what is satirized throughout *Persuasion* is Sir Walter's own complete refusal of sympathy in his cold and complacent self-absorption and devotion to appearances, which encapsulate the failings of his society.

* * *

Yet it is not only through her representation of the older Elliots that Austen treats the issue of personal appearance in *Persuasion*. The narrative of Anne's loss of bloom and her "second spring of youth and beauty" (147) is a powerful and poignant element in the novel. Anne seems entirely to lack the personal vanity of her father and sisters, a lack that is perhaps connected with the long years of neglect within her family that have diminished her sense of her own value. She is represented as acutely and painfully conscious of her changed appearance. The intensity of her awareness of her lost beauty manifests itself in the violence of the language in the free indirect discourse that communicates her thoughts about her looks: her "youth and bloom" are "destroyed," she feels (95); her face is in "ruins" (105).

Through the course of the novel, Anne becomes increasingly a visible presence, in the sense that the other characters, both central and peripheral, are increasingly represented as noticing her and the phases of her fluctuating appearance. Austen scrupulously and pointedly avoids any hint that Anne might share her father's narcissism: "Anne Elliot has no moment of looking at herself, no glance in a mirror or contemplation of any part of her body she might see – she becomes visible in the text only through the comments others make about how she looks," Robin Warhol comments, adding that Anne's body "takes shape then in the objectifying view of other characters, especially male characters" (23). Captain Wentworth at first finds her "'so altered he should not have known her again'" (95), as Mary unkindly informs her sister. At Lyme, however, William Elliot sees her with great admiration – causing Captain Wentworth to look at her with new eyes. Soon after, Lady Russell notes Anne's improvement "in plumpness and looks" (117). Sir Walter shares this view (and typically attributes it to self-preservation with Gowland's lotion). In Molland's confectionery shop in Bath, Wentworth's nameless acquaintances notice her and comment that "'she is pretty, I think, Anne Elliot; very pretty when you come to look at her,'" though "'too delicate'" for most men (196). And, after her renewal of vows with Wentworth at Elizabeth's party, in her happiness she is "more generally admired than she thought about or cared for" (252). Austen carefully indicates that Wentworth's response to Anne's appearance, and Anne's own feelings about her appearance, are merely indications of their intense and shifting relation to each other. When, at the end of the novel, Wentworth claims to Anne, "'in my eye you could never alter,'" Anne is happy to ignore his former contradictory words: she feels that his change of opinion about her looks is "the result not the cause of a revival of his warm attachment" (250). For Anne and for Wentworth physical beauty is associated with love. Austen avoids any implication that either of them shares in the Elliot fetishizing of beauty.

Anne's appearance, then, like her father's and her sister's, is a matter for commentary throughout the novel. But unlike her father she does not look at her own reflection. Moreover, Austen represents Anne's appearance, unlike that of her father or of her sister Elizabeth, as fluctuating. Her body changes because she is, in complete contrast to the rest of her family, a creature of vivid responses. Marilyn Butler, amongst others, has commented on Anne's "abnormally intense experience" and her "high-wrought nervous tension" (278). Mary Waldron describes the language that recounts Anne's reactions to Wentworth as "the unstructured reactions of strong emotion" (143). As many critics have pointed out, she is acutely physically responsive: Judy Van Sickle Johnson speaks of Anne's "deeply felt physical life" ("Bodily Frame" 43), Peter Knox-Shaw of the "unusually physiological quality" of Austen's treatment of Anne (235). Her cheeks burn when she hears of Wentworth (94); the strength of her emotions after reading Wentworth's proposal makes her "very ill" (238).

Jocelyn Harris notes that the *Austen Concordance* adduces 236 instances of "feel or its cognates in *Persuasion*" (142). A stronger and more physically suggestive word, however, is "agitation," and Austen applies this word repeatedly to Anne's intensity of response to Wentworth: renewed agitation, when she first meets him again (60); agitation that is concealed only by Mrs Musgrove's bulk when Anne and Wentworth share a sofa (101); "a confusion of varying, but very painful agitation" when Wentworth relieves her from the tormenting little Walter (112); the "extreme agitation" she feels after she overhears Wentworth's conversation with Louisa (118); the "agitation, pain, pleasure, a something between delight and misery" she experiences when she sees Wentworth in Bath (194); the "restless agitation" the evening before the renewal of her engagement (237); the "agitations" she suffers in the inn before the proposal scene (239); the "fresh agitation" she feels after reading Wentworth's love letter (246). The narrative voice sometimes gently suggests a degree of amusement at Anne's intensities: Anne is at one point described as "deep in the happiness of such misery or the misery of such happiness" (239), but such humor does not really distance the reader from Anne, who is indeed quite capable of laughing at herself.

Anne's responsiveness is not merely solipsistic. She responds to the feelings and needs of other people as well as to her own. She has acquired the skill or grace of attention in her relation to other people. To those like Sir Walter and Elizabeth, to whom the most she can usefully and sincerely offer is courtesy, that is what she gives. Her gifts to others who are more open to receive them are far richer. She has, as the narrative voice informs us, "a great deal of quiet observation" (72) as well as "a quickness of perception […] a nicety in the discernment of character, a natural penetration" (255). This intelligent responsiveness is that of an active participant, not a mere spectator. Her observant sensitivity and sympathy make her an invaluable member of any society – except her own home, that hall of mirrors, where her wider concerns, stricter principles and more general sympathies mean that she is "no good at all" (72), especially in comparison to the flattering Mrs Clay. John Wiltshire stresses the importance of nursing in *Persuasion* and sees Anne's usefulness in these terms.[20] Anne is undoubtedly a good nurse: she can justifiably tell the hypochondriac Mary, "'you know I always cure you when I come'" (75); she is little Charles's best nurse after his fall; and as for the care of Louisa, "'no one so proper, so capable as Anne!'" (141). Her concern for other people, however, includes their psychological as well as their physical suffering. For instance, Anne encourages Captain Benwick to talk about his literary tastes out of "a very good impulse of her nature" (129), but good impulse becomes effective action through a combination of qualities, physical and intellectual. "The engaging mildness of her countenance and the gentleness of her manners" overcome his shyness (129), her literary intelligence arouses him to discuss Byron and Scott, and her wider reading enables her to offer him advice about memoirs, letters and essays. Above all, her sympathetic though tacit acknowledgment of his grief, deepened as it is by fellow-feeling, frees him to express "feelings glad to burst their usual restraints" (129). In this relation as in others, Anne shows her exceptional capacity for attention to other people and the physical, emotional and intellectual gifts that enrich it.

A similar intelligence enables Anne to perceive and to ameliorate where possible the tensions and difficulties in the various social groups of which at various points she is a member, aware as she is of the different demands and assumptions of the various social groupings. She – and she alone – sees the dangerously tangled relationships between Louisa, Henrietta, Wentworth and Charles Hayter, and here she cannot act. But in other cases she is able to "listen patiently, soften every grievance, and excuse each to the other" (82). More effectively, she can comfort the Musgroves during the period of Louisa's illness, so much so that they wonder "what should they do without her? They were wretched comforters for one another" (146). Through a long series of incidents, both major and minor, Austen establishes and validates Anne's responsiveness and activity.

Anne has, in Iris Murdoch's terms, the capacity, apparently both inherent through the nature of her intelligence and acquired through her sense of duty, to see beyond the demands of her own ego and to give her attention to the needs of others. This capacity seems during the course of the novel to have become largely unconscious through habitual use, but it is also a matter of conscious thought and decision. Throughout the novel she is aware of the necessarily different concerns of what she calls each "little social commonwealth" (79) that she enters. She consciously directs her energies towards sharing in the concern of the "commonwealth" in which she finds herself: "With the prospect of spending at least two months at Uppercross, it was highly incumbent on her to clothe her imagination, her memory and all her ideas, in as much of Uppercross as possible" (79). Anne may be naturally responsive to other people; she also deliberately directs her energies – imagination, memory, ideas – towards their concerns.[21] Attention is a matter of will as well as spontaneous impulse.

Anne's fluctuating beauty relates to her responsiveness to the changes and processes of the society that surrounds her.[22] Left to her unsympathetic sister and father at Kellynch, her talents either wasted or unappreciated, unsurprisingly she pines and grows haggard. The stimulus of the various needs of the Musgroves and the renewal of her own emotional life reanimate her physically. Austen carefully provides a contrast in a father and a sister who are "blooming as ever" (49) simply because of the self-absorption that protects them from such hazards to health and beauty as emotion, useful activity, or loving-kindness.

The strongest contrast to Anne is her father, whose self-admiration is more complete than that of Elizabeth, whose position as an unmarried woman makes her uncomfortably aware of the implications of her twenty-nine years. Sir Walter is preserved – freeze-dried – by the coldness that Austen repeatedly ascribes to him and to Elizabeth: their entrance to the Musgroves' rooms at the inn "seemed to give a general chill" and reduces the animated party into "cold composure" (236).[23] Coldness immobilizes. Anne, who moves and is moved, is associated with warmth. Her "spring of felicity" lies in "the warmth of her heart" (258), and she delights in the warmth of others – the Musgroves, the Crofts, the Harvilles: "'God forbid that I should undervalue the warm and faithful feelings of any of my fellow-creatures!'" she exclaims (244). Her pleasure in the external world is not confined to direct human contacts. Austen represents her as a reader of prose, fictional and otherwise, and of poetry, Italian as well as English, as a musician of some ability and as responsive to the natural world at Lyme and Uppercross.

Persuasion includes another character besides the older Elliots whose good looks are unchanging. The years that destroy Anne's "youth and bloom" only give "a more glowing, manly, open look" to Captain Wentworth (95). Wentworth is unchanging in another, less desirable, respect: "he had not forgiven Anne Elliot" (95). He does not question his own judgment. He has not recognized the human necessity of mutability, as is evident in his speech to Louisa about firmness:

> "Here is a nut," said he, catching one down from an upper bough. "To exemplify, – a beautiful glossy nut, which, blessed with original strength, has outlived all the storms of autumn. Not a puncture, not weak spot any where. – This nut," he continued, with playful solemnity, – "while so many of its brethren have fallen and been trodden under foot, is still in possession of all the happiness that a hazel-nut can be supposed capable

of." Then returning to his former earnest tone: "My first wish for all, whom I am interested in, is that they should be firm." (117)

But, of course, a nut must fall to the ground and break, or be broken, in order to fulfill its function.[24] Wentworth's supreme and inflexible self-confidence – the self-confidence that Anne loves and Lady Russell fears – provides him with the same kind of protective carapace that vanity gives to Sir Walter. "'I […] would not understand you, or do you justice,'" he tells Anne (234). Wentworth, during the course of the novel, learns to criticize himself, to understand his own weaknesses, to accept Anne's values, and to be ready for change.

* * *

Persuasion has often been described as an autumnal novel – and so in part it is, both literally and in the sense that autumn is a season of intense awareness of inevitable change.[25] But it is not a novel of one season. This novel is set at a specific historical period, and that in itself suggests the workings of time. The sense of time passing is further suggested by the changing year. Austen always indicates the seasons against which her plots move, but here she seems to emphasize seasonal change – the busyness of mid-autumn with the farmers at work with the plough and nuts hanging from the trees, the darkness of late November, with its "small thick rain almost blotting out the very few objects ever to be discerned" from the window (147), Christmas time with its roaring fires and ongoing winter feasts of "brawn and cold pies" (156), the dismal days of January and February at Bath. Linda Bree's words encapsulate a common critical perception: "*Persuasion* explores questions of loss, change and decay, of impermanence and uncertainty, of risk and chance – all questions that we recognize as endemic in an insecure modern world" (37). But loss, change and decay are a feature of all ages, and the novel never lets its readers forget this.

Austen's treatment of personal appearance in this novel, more so even than her treatment of the seasons, gives the issue of time and change an external physical form. Several characters, notably (but not only) Sir Walter Elliot, are virtually untouched by time, either through self-obsession or through over-confidence. Other characters, however, bear the scars of time, notably (but not only) Anne Elliot. Austen represents these physical changes, unwelcome as they may well be, as the natural outcome of responsiveness, of feeling, of acting and interacting. Those, like Sir Walter, who fail to respond to the world outside themselves are in fact denying their existence as ethical creatures. Anne is represented through much of *Persuasion* as an isolated sensibility in a desert of the unfeeling or the unintelligent. Her fluctuating appearance suggests a responsive and living reality that is central to the values of this novel.

Conclusion

"CREATIVE ATTENTION"

In concluding *Jane Austen's Families*, I turn first to Austen's own endings, for the family continues to play a significant role right into the last pages, even the last sentences, of her novels. These endings show a persistent imaginative engagement with the complex emotional and moral lives of her characters in the context of their communities. While Austen's closing chapters establish the happy marriages that genre and reader expectations require, they also show other elements in the future lives of her central characters, usually emphasizing the ongoing interactions between the heroines and their families or friends, a narrative element that is sometimes overshadowed by the generic satisfactions of the weddings.

The last chapter of *Sense and Sensibility* brings about the necessary two happy marriages for its two heroines. Tellingly, however, its last paragraph is concerned not so much with these marriages as with family relationships, confirming the continuing closeness of the Dashwood family. Although the narrator notes with approval Mrs Dashwood's "prudent" decision to retain an independent home for herself and her youngest daughter in Barton when both her elder daughters live at Delaford, the four women remain interdependent, as they have always been:

> Between Barton and Delaford, there was that constant communication which strong family affection would naturally dictate; – and among the merits and the happiness of Elinor and Marianne, let it not be ranked as the least considerable, that though sisters, and living almost within sight of each other, they could live without disagreement between themselves, or producing coolness between their husbands. (381)

The tone of these closing words of the novel is ironic but the strength and importance of a wider family life is firmly established, emphasized by its final position.

Again in *Pride and Prejudice* the double wedding towards which the narrative has been inexorably leading is established briskly in the first sentence of the last chapter of the novel: "Happy for all her maternal feelings was the day on which Mrs Bennet got rid of her two most deserving daughters" (382). The rest of the chapter deals (rather less ironically) with the ongoing family relationships of Darcy and Elizabeth. Mr Bennet, for instance, missing Elizabeth, delights "in going to Pemberley, especially when he was least expected" (382). Elizabeth helps out Lydia financially and astonishes Georgiana by teasing Mr Darcy. Lady Catherine finds it convenient to forgive her nephew for marrying Elizabeth. More importantly, Austen also establishes the continuance of the loving relationship between Jane and Elizabeth who, after Jane's first year at Netherfield, have "in addition to every other source of happiness" that of living "within thirty miles of each other" (382). And, as with *Sense and Sensibility*, the last words of this novel concern family relationships, in this case with the Gardiners. Austen's emphasis on this relationship is especially significant for it confirms that Darcy, who once found the profession of Elizabeth's uncle "objectionable" (218), has indeed learnt to care more for intelligence, good taste and good manners than for social position. The two couples "were always on the most intimate terms. Darcy as well as Elizabeth really loved them; and they were both ever sensible of the warmest gratitude towards the persons who by bringing her into Derbyshire, had been the means of uniting them" (385). Married happiness, emphasized by that reference to their "warmest gratitude" for bringing them together, is set in the context of family affection.

Mansfield Park too looks beyond the marriage of Fanny and Edmund. Its busy last chapter concludes the stories of all the central characters, but its emphasis is on Fanny's growing happiness and her contentment in all her important relationships, not only that with her husband. Susan Price is happily and usefully established at Mansfield Park and William's "good conduct and rising fame" and the rest of the young Prices' "general well-doing and success" are a source of contentment for both Fanny and her uncle (467). The final pages stress Sir Thomas's affection for Fanny, which grows so strong that "after settling her at Thornton Lacey with every kind attention to her comfort, the object of almost every day was to see her there, or to get her away from it" (467). When finally she and Edmund move to Mansfield the attachment to the family home is reiterated, as Mansfield Parsonage "soon grew as dear to her heart, and as thoroughly perfect in her eyes, as everything else, within the view and patronage of Mansfield Park, had long been" (468). Once again, the closing words of a novel that has represented the difficulties and complexities of family life confirm the value of family bonds.

In *Emma*, as in *Mansfield Park*, the central marriage is endogamous. Fanny marries the cousin with whom she has lived as sister and brother, while Emma marries her sister's brother-in-law and in both cases these marriages are represented as strengthening family ties (which does not always happen in such matches). The continuing physical attachment to the parental home is even stronger in *Emma* than in *Mansfield Park*, as Mr Knightley supports Emma in her filial obligations by living at Hartfield with her father. And the last sentence, once again, both confirms the love of the bride and groom and sets it in the context of the love of a wider group: "the wishes, the hopes, the confidence, the predictions of the small band of true friends who witnessed the ceremony, were fully answered in the perfect happiness of the union" (405).

Only *Northanger Abbey* and *Persuasion* are exceptions to this manner of closing the narrative with the assurance of family ties. No reader of *Northanger Abbey* would bother to doubt Catherine Morland's ongoing attachment to her parents as Catherine Tilney, but it is no concern of the narrator's. *Northanger Abbey* resembles the juvenilia in its exuberant play with literary conventions and expectations, and this play is especially evident in the last chapter as in the first. Various metatextual references – to "the tell-tale compression of the pages" ahead with their message that "we are all hastening together to perfect felicity" (238), to "the rules of composition" (238) in regard to an eligible Viscount suddenly introduced in the closing pages, to the joke about the arguably antisocial "tendency of the work" in the final sentence (239) – all interact to detach both narrator and reader from the fiction.[1] By contrast, *Persuasion* ends with much more emotional involvement in the narrative, yet the only indication of an ongoing relationship with Anne's family comes in an ironic narrative comment about her sister Mary's sufferings "in seeing Anne restored to the rights of seniority and mistress of a very pretty landaulette" (256). As there is no attachment between Anne and her father or her elder sister there is no suggestion of any significant continuing relationship. However, instead of family, Anne has "two friends to add to [Captain Wentworth's] list" (257) and the closing paragraphs accordingly touch on these two friends, again stressing the continuance of old ties as well as the establishment of new. Wentworth learns to value Lady Russell and helps Mrs Smith to recover her West Indian inheritance. In *Persuasion*, as definitely exogamous as *Pride and Prejudice*, friends take the place of family in setting married happiness within a community and bringing the narrative near to its close. In the very last sentence of the novel, however, the focus widens further to the larger community to which Anne now belongs by marriage, and its last words are a tribute to the courage and domestic virtues of the Royal Navy.

Celebration of the new loves and responsibilities that marriage brings join with a confirmation of old loves and responsibilities in the last pages of Austen's novels. The importance of family interactions is evident from their first pages to their last. Although marriage brings unhappiness to many of her characters – to Lady Elliot, for instance, or Mrs Tilney or Mr Bennet – Austen represents it as holding the possibility of personal happiness and fulfilment. She also represents it as a link with a wider community of family and friends.

***

Yet Austen's novels are obviously not narratives of mere continuation. As comedies on the Shakespearean model, they resolve themselves through the elimination of problems, the promise of new life and multiple marriages. *Northanger Abbey*, *Sense and Sensibility*, *Pride and Prejudice* and *Mansfield Park* all end with two marriages, and *Emma* and *Persuasion* end with three – besides all the various marriages that occur within the narratives of all the novels except *Northanger Abbey*.[2] These marriages provide both narrative satisfaction and the sense of a proper resolution.[3] Such satisfaction, however, is not merely a matter of the proper ending of a love story. The release of tension also comes from a sense of relief at the confirmation of the ethical standards to which the heroine has been moving or which she has with difficulty been maintaining throughout the narrative. The introduction to this book quotes a phrase of Simone Weil's, "creative attention," words that apply to Austen's work both in relation to the choices she makes as an artist and in the choices she represents her characters as making. All her protagonists are, to various extents, capable of a careful and minute regard for the needs and preoccupations of other people. Such attention becomes increasingly effective and increasingly necessary with greater knowledge, the kind of intimacy that is often fostered within a family. For Elinor Dashwood, for example, concern for the comfort of Mrs Jennings demands some effort but only a very general attention, and despite her preoccupations – anxiety over Marianne, unhappiness over Edward, reluctance to go to London – that is what she offers in the carriage journey from Barton to Mrs Jennings' house near Portman Square: "Elinor took immediate possession of the post of civility which she had assigned herself, behaved with the greatest attention to Mrs Jennings, talked with her, laughed with her, and listened to her *whenever she could*" (185 – emphasis added). In regard to Marianne, however, Elinor's attention is more finely tuned.[4] In her loving concern for her sister's wellbeing, for instance, she stifles her own bitterness against Willoughby, "lest she might wound Marianne still deeper by treating their disengagement [...] as an escape from the worst and most irremediable of all evils" (205). Again, when she tells Marianne about Willoughby's apology, she breaks the news with scrupulous care for Marianne's health and happiness: "she managed the recital, as she hoped, with address; prepared her anxious listener with caution; related simply and honestly the chief points on which Willoughby grounded his apology; did justice to his repentance, and softened only his protestations of present regard" (352). Through such details of behaviour, representations of minute moral choices evident in all her novels, Austen communicates an ethics of ordinary life. Characters such as Elinor Dashwood, Fanny Price and Anne Elliot – and Mr Knightley – exercise creative attention in often difficult circumstances throughout their narratives. Marianne Dashwood, Elizabeth Bennet and Emma Woodhouse – and Mr Darcy – come to exercise it more fully and generously in the course of their narratives. In every case, Austen represents their marriages as providing a wider world for their exercise of creative attention.

***

"Creative attention" is certainly a phrase that applies to Austen herself as an artist. Throughout her novels, her concern with the necessity for observant and intelligent care in human interactions (and the comedy involved in the failure of such care) is paralleled in her care for accuracy in every relevant social and material detail. To some extent this precision is a matter of genre. As one who eschews the Sentimental and the Gothic in her own fiction (apart from the joyful satire on these modes in the juvenilia and *Northanger Abbey*), and who turns instead to nature and probability in her version of realism, accuracy of various kinds is essential. But her choice of genre in itself is also a matter of respect, and indeed relish, for what is, for the world with which she was presented. This care for accuracy is the basis of Peter Graham's comparison between Austen and Charles Darwin; as he asserts, "they look with scrupulous, penetrating, and relatively unbiased attention at the rich and messy details of the world around them" (2).[5] Austen's "naturalist's" eye is trained on human specimens and therefore she is scrupulous in representing human contexts. Her advice on the novel that her niece Anna Austen was writing shows the importance that Austen attaches to a minute care for detail, both in the closeness with which she read Anna's work and in the nature and multiplicity of the problems she notes. Her suggested revisions involve such matters as consistency of characterization, matters of propriety, questions of etiquette (a country surgeon would not, apparently, be introduced to a man of rank),[6] likely topics of conversation and suitable language ("Bless my Heart" is "too familiar & inelegant" for a particular character). At the same time she warns Anna against useless details in physical description – "too many particulars of right and left."[7]

Austen certainly omits unnecessary details in her own fiction. We know little about her characters' appearance or their dress. Nor do we know much more about the houses in which they find themselves. It is for such as Mr Collins to enumerate the number of windows on the façade at Rosings. Because of the sparsity of material details, the few that are included are all the more telling – the glare of the sun on the greasy marks left by the head of Mr Price on the walls at Portsmouth (*MP* 438), for instance, or the glass of Constantia wine that Mrs Jennings offers as a remedy for Marianne's misery, remembering how good it was for her late husband's "cholicky gout" (*S&S* 218). Austen's concern to represent accurately whatever she chooses to represent is the basis for her suggestion to Anna Austen that she should not actually show her characters in Ireland, a country of which Anna had no experience: "You will be in danger of giving false representations," she comments (*Letters* 269). One sees her at work on such details in her letter to Cassandra, asking her to check on whether Northamptonshire was "a Country of Hedgerows" (*Letters* 202) when she was working on *Mansfield Park*.[8]

However, Austen's accuracy is largely a matter of character, as it expresses itself through speech, movement and personal interactions. In every novel the closeness and attention with which Austen has imagined her characters is apparent in their idiolect, as J. F. Burrows' study shows. The warmth and playfulness of the Musgrove family are immediately apparent in Charles Musgrove's announcement in the inn at Bath that he has made arrangements for an outing for the family group: "Well, Mother, I have done something for you that you will like. I have been to the theatre and secured a box for tomorrow night. An't I a good boy? I know you love a play; and there is room for us all" (234–5). The characters are fully imagined in their movement too. Before he speaks to his mother, Charles sees some visitors off from the hotel: "the visitors took their leave; and Charles having civilly seen them off […] then made a face at them and abused them for coming" (234), which fully communicates Charles's good manners, his boyishness, strong sense of his own preferences and love of the family circle. Similarly in *Pride and Prejudice*, when the two sisters run to find out about Mr Bennet's letter from Mr Gardiner about Lydia, their physical and psychological differences are immediately apparent through their movement: "Jane who was not so light, nor so much in the habit of running as Elizabeth, soon lagged behind, while her sister, panting for breath came up with him" (309). Yet any single example falsifies by selecting one facet of Austen's attentive accuracy from the rest. In every scene the interaction between characters in a particular setting, whether it is a hot day at Box Hill or a private ball at Netherfield Park, is fully imagined. In her fiction, Austen shows the same complete focus on the subject that at their best her protagonists show in their relations with other people – the same "creative attention." To approach Austen, whether as a reader, a critic or a teacher, through the lens of ethical criticism, through an alertness to her complex representations of moral choice in ordinary domestic interactions, illuminates virtually every aspect of her art.

***

Austen's personal experience of the interactions and oddities of family life within the social groups she chose to write about was large and varied. She knew about the stresses and pleasures of family life through her own birth family of eight children, through the families her brothers James, Edward, Francis and Charles produced, through the lives of "the great web of cousins," to quote Tomalin (4), on both sides of the family, through good neighbours such as the Lefroys and the Lloyds. She witnessed or experienced many of the general situations she writes about: the child adopted into a richer family (as her brother Edward was); the clever younger sister dependent on and admiring of an elder (as Jane relied on Cassandra); the power and responsibility the death of a mother can heap on the shoulders of the eldest available daughter (a situation her niece Fanny Austen experienced at the age of fifteen); the possible frictions within a household that includes the children of two wives (such as that of James Austen before his elder daughter Anna's marriage). In her published work, while she draws on all this wealth of potential material, she transforms it through the power of her imagination acting on the product of her acute and unflinching attention to human reactions and interactions.[9]

NOTES

General Introduction

1 The one exception is Catharine in *Catharine, or The Bower*, which Austen wrote when she was seventeen. It begins playfully: "Catharine had the misfortune, as many heroines have had before her, of losing her parents when she was very young" (186).
2 Jane Nardin, amongst others, points out the absence of this narrative device ("Children and their Families" 73).
3 In a letter to Cassandra, 11–12 October 1813, Austen writes about Mary Brunton's *Self-Control* as "an excellently-meant, elegantly-written Work, without anything of Nature or Probability in it. I declare I do not know whether Laura's passage down the American River is not the most natural, possible, every-day thing she ever does" (*Letters* 234).
4 A possible exception is *Persuasion*: Anne, whose loving nature is demonstrated through her attachment to the memory of her mother, is kind to Mary but can hardly find her an adequate companion. Mary Poovey asserts that Austen fails to account for the differences between siblings in her novels (201) and James Thompson seems to agree with her (111). But at every point Austen provides some indication of why a sibling might be different (position in family, resemblance to mother rather than father). According to current theories of family structure siblings differ according to Darwin's principle of divergence, as Frank Sulloway argues (85). He discusses the question of siblings finding their "niche" within the family at length (83–118). See also Dunn and Plomin.
5 Mary Waldron notes the implications of this ending (35).
6 *Coelebs* rapidly went through numerous editions and inadvertently spawned several sequels and spin-offs, at least three of which were published in the very next year, 1809: *Celia in Search of a Husband; A Sequel to Coelebs* (Fr Barlow); *Coelebs Suited* (George Rover); *Coelibia Choosing a Husband: A Modern Novel* (Robert Torrens). Other Coelebiana listed in the British Library catalogue include *Coelebs Married* (1814), *Coelebs Deceived* (1817), *Coelebs in Search of a Cook* (1860) and *Coelebs the Younger in Search of a Wife* (1859).
7 As Julia Prewitt Brown writes, "Austen's heroines *live* by contradiction and master it" ("Feminist Depreciation" 304).
8 Examples include Tobin Siebers, Robert Miles and Roger Gard. Gard writes, "Jane Austen is obviously one of the most challenging moralists in European fiction and one of its most brilliantly accomplished practitioners" (2). This approach to Austen began as early as 1821, when Richard Whately wrote, "the moral lessons […] of this lady's novels though clearly and impressively conveyed, are not offensively put forward, but spring incidentally from the circumstances of the story; they are not forced upon the reader, but he is left to collect them (though without any difficulty) for himself; her's [*sic*] is that unpretending kind of instruction which is furnished by real life; and certainly no author has ever conformed more closely to real life, as well as in the incidents, as in the characters and descriptions" (95).

9 Richard Rorty argues that in such a post-philosophical period as he looks forward to "we would view the novel rather than the treatise as the genre in which the European intellect comes to fruition" ("Comment" 27). He is not talking about ethics as such, though, but rather arguing for the greater and more appropriate communicative power of discourse possible in fiction. Similarly, Nussbaum says that Proust and James both claim that "only the style of a certain kind of narrative artist (and not for instance the style associated with the abstract theoretical treatise) can adequately state certain important truths about the world" (*Love's Knowledge* 6).

10 I share S. L. Goldberg's feelings about Murdoch. He writes: "My argument [...] owes a great deal to Iris Murdoch's *The Sovereignty of Good* – a book which so deepened my understanding of the moral aspects of literature that my debts to it are now too basic and too pervasive to be spelt out in detail" (253). David Parker also pays tribute to "the pioneering work of Iris Murdoch which so subtly extends the sphere of the ethical" (*Ethics* 98).

11 Tobin Siebers points out the relevance of Bingley's insisting that in the discussion of hypothetical cases one needs "all the particulars," teasing Darcy as being "a great tall fellow, who can easily command deference" (150).

12 Siebers, referring to Alasdair MacIntyre's *After Virtue*, notes, "Austen represents for [MacIntyre] one of the last great imaginative voices of the tradition of thought concerned with the theory and practice of virtue. Everything tends to be particular within her world. She writes about individuals, living with others, being changed and challenged by them" (Siebers 49–50).

13 More's contempt for the novel actually spurred her into writing fiction: "I thought there were already good books enough in the world for good people; but that there was a large class of people whose wants had not been attended to; –the subscribers to the circulating library [i.e. novel readers]. A little to raise the tone of that mart of mischief, and to counteract its corruptions I thought was an object worth attempting" (Roberts 3.313–4). More's admirers understood *Coelebs* similarly. The Bishop of Lincoln seems to be referring to fiction when he writes to More: "I could not but feel a strong conviction that a work, so excellent in its principles and so entertaining in its nature must be in an eminent degree useful, to a class of readers in particular, who seldom take up a book but to derive mischief from it" (Roberts 3. 325). See also Nardin, "Jane Austen, Hannah More." For contemporary defences of the novel see Harris 22–4.

14 Johnson's opposition to "mixed characters," such as those of Henry Fielding, is most fully expressed in *Rambler* 4: "many characters ought never to be drawn," he asserts there (30).

15 Sabina Lovibond, in a stimulating discussion of Murdoch as a philosopher, discusses the disturbing possibility that Murdoch follows Weil into a "*de facto* celebration of the 'feminine' moral position" (86).

16 Nussbaum mentions Murdoch's *The Sovereignty of Good*, which includes the essay to which I refer, "The Idea of Perfection."

17 Cora Diamond speaks of Nussbaum's claim that "there are some moral views that can be adequately expressed only through novels" (39). One might compare Richard Rorty, who writes, "this process of coming to see other human beings as 'one of us' rather than as 'them' is a matter of detailed description of what unfamiliar people are like and of redescription of what we ourselves are. This is not a task for theory but for genres such as ethnography, the journalists' report, the comic book, the docudrama, and especially the novel" (*Contingency* xvi).

18 John Wiltshire says that in *Pride and Prejudice* Austen's comic characters "have no meaningful interaction with the outside world of others' feelings" (*Recreating* 103). This is both an artistic and a moral point: they are less than fully human because they cannot see beyond themselves.
19 Linda Hutcheon refers to "palimpsestuous" as Michael Alexander's "great term," and goes on, "if we know this prior text we always feels its presence shadowing the one we are experiencing directly" (6).

Part I   Introduction

1 *The Way of All Flesh* was written in the early 1870s, but was not published until 1903. I have borrowed this quotation from Mary Burgan (552).

Chapter One   The Functions of the Dysfunctional Family: *Northanger Abbey*, *Sense and Sensibility*, *Pride and Prejudice*

1 *The Birth of Tragedy* 39–40, 84–5.
2 Austen provides Hill with all the epigraphs to the chapters of this novel, which is also full of Austenian allusions and ends, like *Emma*, with three pairings. Hill's 2008 novel *A Cure for All Diseases* is based on Austen's unfinished *Sanditon*.
3 Mary Waldron usefully quotes Mary Russell Mitford's comment that Austen "wants nothing but the beau-ideal of the female character to be a perfect novel-writer" (4).
4 Tony Tanner writes of Fanny Price that "she is never, ever, wrong" (*Jane Austen* 143*)*. However, as Mary Waldron argues, "all Austen's major characters – yes, even Fanny Price and Mr Knightley – are morally inconsistent, threading their way through conflicting courses through which there proves to be no systematic guide" (14). Janet Todd has usefully divided Fanny's critics into three groups: "the hostile ones, who find her distasteful or nauseating […] the approving critics, who find Fanny the true embodiment of the ideals of the novel […] the ironic critics, who consider Fanny intentionally flawed" (*Women's Friendship* 246).
5 Wikipedia defines a dysfunctional family as one in which "conflict, misbehaviour, or even abuse, on the part of individual members occur continually, leading other members to accommodate such actions." Wikipedia, "Dysfunctional family." Online: http://en.wikipedia.org/wiki/Dysfunctional_family. Accessed 6 November 2012.
6 Butler is writing here of another Catharine, the heroine of Austen's early attempt at serious fiction, *Catharine, or the Bower*. (Austen spells the names differently in the two novels.)
7 The language used of the Morlands is interesting in light of Peter Knox-Shaw's observation that this novel is full of such phrases as "the natural course of things," "the ordinary course of life" (117).
8 Kenneth Moler usefully compares what Ann Radcliffe writes in *The Castles of Athlin and Dunbayn*: "When first we enter on the theatre of the world […] the happy benevolence of our feelings prompts us to believe that every body is good" (*Art of Allusion* 22). Benedict and Le Faye point out that Catherine is the only one of Austen's heroines who leaves home and meets her future husband "in some hitherto unknown location" (lx).
9 Jane Nardin writes, "away from home, Catherine encounters a series of people who cannot be judged adequately on the basis of her parents' assumptions about life" ("Children and their Families" 74).

10 Juliet McMaster points out that James Morland is "brought up in the same unsophisticated matter-of-fact speech practices" as Catherine, and still at the end of the novel retains some illusions about Isabella Thorpe (*Jane Austen Novelist* 212).
11 Rachel Brownstein argues, "that Catherine does not in fact change or learn very much – her mind being, first and last, 'warped by an innate principle of general integrity,' in Henry Tilney's wry formulation – is an ironic comment on novels of education" (*Cambridge Companion* 37).
12 Henry Tilney's pedantry is shown in his commentaries on the words "amazingly," "nice" (121) and "promise faithfully" (193); his fantasy is shown in the Gothic romance he concocts for Catherine on the way to Northanger (161–3), in his imaginings about Catherine's journals (51) and his comparison of dancing partners with marriage partners (95–6), for instance.
13 The most notorious outpouring of dislike for Fanny as priggish is probably Kingsley Amis's "What Became of Jane Austen." In 1917, Reginald Farrer described Fanny as a "prig-pharisee" (24).
14 Mary Waldron comments, "it is here that Gothic fantasy and real life mesh for Catherine; for the first time her reading is her only guide" (31).
15 Robert Miles suggests that Catherine must learn she is a character in a novel rather than in a Gothic romance – or rather that life combines "Romance and Novel" (75).
16 Eleanor says to Catherine, "'you must have been long enough in this house to see that I am but a nominal mistress of it, that my real power is nothing.'" She has also to acknowledge that her father's temper is "'not happy'" (217).
17 Joe Wright, the director of this adaptation, speaks of Mrs Bennet as "an amazing mother" (meaning evidently "an amazingly good mother"). Deborah Moggach, the writer of the screenplay, speaks of Mrs Bennet as "a heroic character." All the comments from the cast in this DVD special feature suggest the family unity of the Bennets ("A Bennet Family Portrait"). A scene of the Bennet parents in bed is introduced, and Mrs Bennet justifies her matchmaking by a lecture to Elizabeth on the economic position of women. The BBC/A & E version, on the other hand, exaggerates the awfulness of Mrs Bennett with an uncharacteristically unsubtle performance by Alison Steadman. (I recognize that adaptations should be judged on their own merits rather than as versions of their originals). For further discussion, see the articles by Seeber and myself in *Persuasions On-Line*.
18 One of Austen's most acute Victorian critics, Richard Simpson, comments on her representations of strange pairings within marriage: "Now these people are almost always represented as living together in fair comfort; and yet there is scarcely a single pair of them who have not, on the novelist's usual scale of propriety, been woefully mismatched. Sense and stupidity, solidity and frivolity, are represented as in everyday life cosily uniting and making up the elements of a home with the usual average of happiness and comfort" (245).
19 Isobel Armstrong says of Austen, "her novels are saturated in sexual feeling in an almost brazen way" (127). Juliet McMaster discusses this subject at length in *Jane Austen on Love*. Also relevant is Jan Fergus's article, "Sex and Social Life in Jane Austen's Novels."
20 The contrast between the Bennet parents at the news of Elizabeth's engagement is striking. Mr Bennet, once convinced of Elizabeth's love for Darcy, asserts, "'I could not have parted with you, my Lizzy, to any one less worthy'" (376). Mrs Bennet claims Elizabeth, usually "the least dear to her of all her children" (135) as "'my sweetest Lizzy'" and "'my dearest child'" (377) only when she is about to marry money, and is happy to have "got rid" of her two eldest children (382).

21 Austen's reference to Gisborne (*Letters* 112) does not make it clear which of his many publications she had been reading, though it was probably the *Enquiry*. I thank one of the anonymous readers for Anthem Press for pointing out this uncertainty.
22 Karl Kroeber sees Mr Bennet as suffering from "psychological self-injury" and "profound self-disgust" (153).
23 In *Pride and Prejudice* the two eldest children seem to have benefited from the father's genes and possibly their position as the eldest and therefore the most carefully tended of the family, while the three younger inherit their mother's silliness. As poor Mary turns out plain this silliness is forced into commonplace bookishness and "accomplishments." The two youngest sisters provide a sort of parody of the affection between the two eldest. Jane and Elizabeth obviously care greatly for each other as is shown in their words and deeds. Elizabeth wants to think of Jane as "perfect," and as "angelic" (164). Lydia and Kitty, on the other hand, are quite capable of being jealous of each other and resenting each other's good fortune. It should be noted too that there is a strong resemblance between Lydia and Elizabeth in their physical energy and social courage.
24 Robert Miles describes *Sense and Sensibility* as being full of "pairs, doubles, contrasts and reversals" (82).
25 Kenneth Moler discusses other comparison novels in which the contrasts are rather simpler (*Art of Allusion* 46–56). Marilyn Butler and Mary Waldron both emphasize the parallels between *Sense and Sensibility* and other contrast novels, referring to Maria Edgeworth's "The Letters of Julia and Caroline" and Jane West's *A Gossip's Story*. Waldron describes them as "oppositional courtship novels" (78).
26 Isobel Armstrong says, "this seriousness differentiates the Dashwood women as a family from everyone else in the novel" (41).
27 Isobel Armstrong 13.
28 Tony Tanner writes of Mr Bennet's relation to Elizabeth, "this is parenthood as narcissism" (*Jane Austen* 209).
29 Wendy S. Jones comments that "Marianne's traumatic experience with Willoughby is due largely to the lack of intervention from her mother who fails to exert her authority where appropriate" and describes Mrs Dashwood as "a somewhat foolish and overly tolerant mother" (103).

Chapter Two   Spoilt Children: *Pride and Prejudice, Mansfield Park* and *Emma*

1 John Wiltshire points out how long Austen took to write the novel and publish it ("Introduction" xxv–xxxi). She started work on *Mansfield Park* in February 1811 and began work on revising *Pride and Prejudice* in October of the same year, so clearly she was thinking of the two novels together. Margaret Kirkham writes that *First Impressions* had been "extensively and recently revised" before its publication as *Pride and Prejudice* by an author "already thinking of *Mansfield Park*" (91). Jan Fergus thinks it possible that Austen published *Sense and Sensibility* first because it required less revision than *Pride and Prejudice* (129). Pat Rogers, in his introduction to *Pride and Prejudice*, argues that the "adjustments to be made in 1809–10 may have amounted to fine tuning rather than the drastic overhaul some have supposed" (xxx). Certainly Austen writes of having "lopt & cropt" *Pride and Prejudice* (*Letters* 202).

2 An anonymous reviewer in *The British Critic* in February 1813 said of Elizabeth Bennet, "there seems no defect in the portrait" (482).
3 Many other critics, including Kenneth Moler, have perceived that "Mary is, in all essential respects, very nearly Elizabeth's antithesis" (*Art of Allusion* 131).
4 Austen's older contemporary, Amelia Opie, explores in *Adeline Mowbray* (1803) the ways in which Adeline's mother is spoilt by her parents' treatment of her natural advantages and how the spoiling of one generation adversely affects the next generation.
5 Claudia Johnson observes that in being "conceited and inattentive to the feelings of others," Darcy resembles to an extraordinary degree a far less intelligent character, Mr Collins (*Jane Austen* 77). Janis Stout sees in the first proposal "an egotism only a little less extreme than Collins's" (35).
6 Marilyn Butler mentions Jane West's *The Advantages of Education*, Elizabeth Inchbald's *A Simple Story*, Fanny Burney's *Camilla*, Amelia Opie's *Adeline Mowbray*, and Hannah More's *Coelebs in Search of a Wife* in this connection (219). Kenneth Moler, in his discussion of *Mansfield Park*, writes of the contemporary concern with women's education and especially the negative view of the emphasis on women's accomplishment. He refers, in this regard, to Elizabeth Hamilton in *Popular Essays* (1812), Thomas Gisborne's *Enquiry into the Duties of the Female Sex* (1797) Hannah More's *Strictures on the Modern System of Female Education* (1799) and *Coelebs in Search of a Wife* (1808) (*Art of Allusion* 112).
7 Barbara J. Horwitz comments that "Locke is certain that the most serious problems of adulthood are caused by spoiling children" (21).
8 Gene Koppel sees humility as meaning that "one recognizes the limits of the claims of one's ego" (53).
9 Peter Knox-Shaw points out that the Malthusian idea of "the struggle for existence" is very much alive in *Mansfield Park* (174).
10 Roger Gard suggests another reason for Emma's difficulties in the larger community. He believes that this clouding of the intelligence is related to what he calls the "desperately dull society" and "demoralizing tedium" of Highbury (156).
11 Opinions about Darcy's superior good looks, however, may be the result of rumours of his superior wealth. The relation between narrative comment and Meryton gossip is not clear at this point (49).
12 Marilyn Butler comments, "Maria Bertram especially is a girl according to the female moralists' common formula. Having demonstrated her vanity and superficiality in adolescence, she grows up with the typical ambition of marrying for money" (221).
13 Mary Waldron has commented on the frequency with which the combination of wealth and beauty endangers the heroines of eighteenth-century novels, making them "vulnerable to material indulgence and personal vanity, as well as to predatory suitors" (113). As Waldron notes, Emma's temptations are rather different.
14 Claudia Johnson writes of "the family circle" as something that "Austen's more attractive patricians learn to outgrow" (*Jane Austen* 119).
15 Matthew 25.29 (Authorized Version). Mary Burgan writes of the "Dantean force" of their punishment (547). Sir Thomas's harsh treatment of his daughter accords with that suggested by Hannah More: "be not anxious to restore the forlorn penitent to that society against whose laws she has so grievously offended [...] To restore a criminal to public society is perhaps to tempt her to repeat her crime, or to deaden her repentance for having committed it, as well as to injure that society; while to restore a strayed soul to God will add lustre to your Christian character and brighten your eternal crown" (*Strictures* 55).

Chapter Three "Usefulness and Exertion": Mothers and Sisters in *Sense and Sensibility*, *Mansfield Park*, *Emma* and *Persuasion*

1. Janet Todd and Linda Bree, in their introduction to the Cambridge *Later Manuscripts*, outline the arguments for various dates of composition for *Lady Susan*, but comment that they are "inclined to agree" with the family tradition of a date of 1794–45 (liii).
2. Todd and Bree quote the comment of Sandra Gilbert and Susan Gubar in *The Madwoman in the Attic* (169–70) that Lady Susan is one of a number of energetic and powerful mothers in Austen's canon "who seek to destroy their docile children" (lx).
3. In the incomplete *The Watsons* the central character, Emma Watson, is doubly bereaved. Her mother (about whose competence we have no information) dies when Emma is five, and when she is nineteen, the beloved aunt who has adopted her makes a foolish second marriage thus depriving Emma both of her home and her expected inheritance.
4. Fergus sees *Sense and Sensibility* as being an exception to Austen's normal practice in this respect (*Jane Austen* 89).
5. Tave's discussion of exertion as a value in Austen's work focuses on Elinor Dashwood (98–115).
6. David Spring proposes this term, pseudo-gentry, for those who, like Austen's father, were dependent upon, but regarded themselves as virtually equal to, the landed gentry (53–72).
7. In less affluent pseudo-gentry households the mistress of the house might be responsible for the care of the dairy and poultry-yard. Maggie Lane in her article on "Food" in *Jane Austen in Context* notes that Jane Austen's mother had "three cows and ducks, chickens, guinea-fowl and turkeys" (262). Elinor is seen as concerned about the pasturage of her cows after her marriage to Edward Ferrars (*S&S* 376).
8. Elizabeth Langland discusses these responsibilities in some detail, focusing on a slightly later period, in her second chapter.
9. Edward Copeland notes that while in pseudo-gentry households women are responsible for household management, "they are prevented by law from exercising any significant control over the management of the family's income, a male prerogative. If money affairs go wrong […] the woman is still responsible for the economic consequences" (*Cambridge Companion* 137). Judging from the difference between the family's economic position when Lady Elliot was running the household and the position under Elizabeth's control, the woman did have some effective control over money matters. The Elliots are a gentry family: perhaps Lady Elliot had imbibed what Copeland calls "the prudent economic principles of Austen's own class" (*Cambridge Companion* 137).
10. Deborah Kaplan quotes this passage (30) in her discussion of domesticity in genteel life of the period (17–42). She comments on the devotion to her children's education shown by Austen's sister-in-law Elizabeth (31).
11. Graham comments on the differentiated relationship between Anne and Mary: "Mary, growing up junior to a responsibility-shouldering, self-effacing paragon, has thereby been enabled to cultivate self-centered discontent and valetudinarianism." He adds that Mary, unlike Elizabeth, is humanized, perhaps because she is not a beauty, has married into a warm family and has children (77).
12. Wiltshire in the notes to his edition of *Mansfield Park* comments on Mrs Price's maternal affection as an example of Austen once again "recording the limitations of feeling as a source of moral capacity" (724).

13 The findings of recent psychological and sociological research are relevant here. Frank Sulloway comments on the difference between lower class and middle class children who are bereaved of a parent. Lower class children do not lose confidence because they take on new responsibilities: "The gain in personal power" at the loss of a parent becomes "increased extraversion." This phenomenon does not occur in middle class children (Sulloway 190–91).
14 Eleanor Tilney is only nominally the mistress of the house, given her father's insistence on complete control.
15 As Terry Castle points out, "this is a world […] full of motherless or unmothered children – not just Emma but also Frank Churchill, Jane Fairfax, and Harriet Smith, of whose mother nothing is ever known" ("Introduction" xxii). This fact hardly darkens the central narrative at all.
16 Even at Donwell Abbey Emma is hospitable, offering Frank Churchill food and drink as a means of curing his bad temper. Maggie Lane deals with the importance of food in *Emma* in her article on Food in *Jane Austen in Context*, noting that it shows us "the interdependence of the village community" (267).
17 Mansfield Park is a novel of "what-ifs." We are asked to imagine the possibility of Edmund married to Mary Crawford and Fanny married to Henry Crawford and to understand that both of these options might have worked very well.
18 Stuart Tave notes the biblical origin of Henry's remark (169).
19 *Persuasions* 33 (2011) includes a number of strong essays on Mrs Dashwood, including those by Susan Allen Ford and Kathryn Davis.
20 Graham says that Elinor is pushed into attitudes by her "cheerful and sanguine" parents. "Elinor takes it upon herself to provide the substitute for, rather than the junior embodiment of, parental seriousness" (77).
21 Armstrong discusses the difference between the two sisters in relation to their different aesthetic beliefs, Marianne preferring the wildness of the picturesque and Elinor the beauty of usefulness (62).
22 Sarah Emsley discusses the gradual progress of Marianne's change of behaviour (78).
23 The words of the priest summoning communicants to the altar rail according to the 1662 *Book of Common Prayer* (the Anglican prayer book in use in Austen's England) are as follows: "Ye that do truly and earnestly repent you of your sins and are in love and charity with your neighbours and intend to lead a new life following the commandments of God; Draw near with faith". All these words apply to Marianne at this point in her life.
24 Maggie Lane says that Mrs Morland is "the only competent mother of a heroine in the six novels" and adds, "no wonder she has to be kept out of the way" ("The French Bread at Northanger" 136).

Part II   Introduction

1 Tony Tanner provides a summary of the failings of fathers in Austen's novels (*Jane Austen* 45–6).
2 Mary Burgan writes at length about Austen's "implied critique of the patriarchal hierarchy as a proper foundation for social organization" (537).
3 Darryl Jones becomes quite excited about Mr Woodhouse's demerits, describing him as "a pampered, whingeing, cretinous leech – a one-man justification for the class war and literature's best advert for compulsory euthanasia. In fact, I'd happily kill him myself, given the chance" (157).

4 There may be some truth in Lionel Trilling's assertion that "of all the fathers of Jane Austen's novels, Sir Thomas is the only one to whom admiration is given" (226), but the admiration is very diluted.
5 Margaret Kirkham thinks that Mr Woodhouse is "a much worse influence on his daughter than is Harriet Smith" (125).

Chapter Four Money, Morals and *Mansfield Park*

1 Julia Prewitt Brown notes that "all the novels involve three generations, past, present and future" ("Feminist Depreciation" 307).
2 Dr Grant conveniently dies, allowing the living of Mansfield to pass to Edmund just after Edmund and Fanny have been "married long enough to begin to want an increase of income, and feel their distance from the paternal abode an inconvenience" (468). This comment seems to suggest that Fanny has or expects a child. Both Jenkyns (130) and Selwyn (215) note this possibility. Burgan assumes that Austen never hints at the heroine of her novels bearing children (551), as does James Thompson, who sees this as an indication of "the collapse or the constriction of the family in Austen's narrative" (209).
3 This negative relationship between the generations applies also to the play within the novel. In *Lovers' Vows*, Baron Wildenhaim is ignorant of his son's existence, and is threatened by that son, while he is trying to force his daughter into marriage with the rich but corrupt Count Cassel.
4 Leona Toker provides an important discussion of the issue of "conspicuous leisure" in *Mansfield Park*, using Thorstein Veblen's *The Theory of the Leisure Class* (1900) as a partial basis for her argument.
5 In addition, as John Wiltshire points out, "*Mansfield Park* is a novel in whose first volume dramatic ensemble scenes predominate and in which the life of its heroine is marginalized" (*Body* 67).
6 Deidre Lynch, discussing the unfinished *The Watsons*, describes Austen's Emma Watson as isolated "in her moral cognitive individuality" (213). This comment might well be applied to Fanny Price too.
7 Both Dorothy McMillan and Anne Toner discuss the ways in which the ha-ha – the invisible barrier within the estate of a wealthy family – symbolizes Fanny's position as a family member who is nevertheless a perpetual outsider at Mansfield Park.
8 Kenneth Moler argues that the contrast is not entirely flattering to Fanny: "While others in the novel – Sir Thomas, Mary Crawford – are overly worldly, attaching excessive importance to such things as money, rank and their appurtenances, Fanny goes to an opposite extreme, and in the naiveté of a too cloistered virtue closes her eyes to the socio-economic complexities of real life" ("Two Voices" 173).
9 Q. D. Leavis argues that *Mansfield Park* is a re-working of "Lady Susan," in which the contrast between London values and those of the country gentry is significant. See especially page 32.
10 In this regard, Wiltshire comments on the careful use of characteristic Northamptonshire place names.
11 Dickens's concern is especially apparent in *Little Dorrit*, from which I quote, and in *A Christmas Carol*.
12 I discuss Austen's relation to Yonge elsewhere, focusing on *Emma* ("*Emma* in the 1860s" 327–30; *Heaven* 61–7). The plot of *Heartsease* may be summarized as follows: A young, timid, but highly-principled and religious girl from a large, humble family is taken

into a rich, upper-class household, whose money comes mainly from estates in the West Indies. In this cold and formal family, she is neglected, snubbed and made to feel like a vulgar and uneducated outsider, especially by the beautiful but passive lady of the house, by a self-possessed daughter of the house – and most of all by a spiteful, hostile and mercenary aunt. One of the two sons shows her great kindness, but she suffers greatly through a number of trials and is often unwell. She is brought into direct rivalry for the affections of her beloved with a richer, livelier and better-born young woman. Eventually, after a series of family disasters, her strict adherence to her own ethical code places her as the moral centre of her household, a household that is made more humane by her central role in it. (This summary is directed at underlining the resemblance between the two novels.)

13 Like the Bertrams, the Martindales of *Heartsease* own property on a Leeward Island, but theirs is on Barbuda rather than Antigua.

14 Isobel Armstrong contrasts Austen with Yonge, pointing out that too moralistic a reading is simplistic: "To accept this is to think of her texts as if they were the ideologically closed writings of a novelist such as Charlotte Yonge (another Anglican conservative)" (123).

15 In order to communicate the morally unstable basis of life at Mansfield Park, Patricia Rozema, in her film, emphasizes the issue of slavery, about which twentieth-century audiences would have strong and predictable reactions. Austen's treatment of money would be more difficult to communicate visually, while the relevant figures (of income and so on) would mean little to Rozema's audience.

16 Edward Said's article, which appeared initially in *Raymond Williams: Critical Perspectives* (Ed. Terry Eagleton. Boston: Northeastern University Press, 1989: 150–64) reappeared in *Culture and Imperialism* in 1994.

17 She is, of course, playfully misquoting Scott (*Marmion* 6.38).

18 The many discussions of slavery and *Mansfield Park* include Moira Ferguson's in *Subject to Others: British Women Writers and Colonial Slavery, 1670–1834*; Maaya Stewart's in *Domestic Realities and Imperial Fictions: Jane Austen's Novels in Eighteenth Century Contexts*; Judith Terry's in "Sir Thomas Bertram's Business"; Suvendrini Perera's in *Reaches of Empire: The English Novel from Edgeworth to Dickens*; John Wiltshire's in "Decolonising Mansfield Park."

19 The extremely disturbing Blake illustration in question (from John Stedman's *Narrative of a Five Years' Expedition against the Revolted Negroes of Surinam*) is captioned "A Negro hung alive by the Ribs to a Gallows" (reproduced Ackroyd 170). In Rozema's screenplay, it is presented as part of Tom Bertram's Antigua sketchbook and labeled "Equiano's Last Day" (128). Other illustrations from the sketchbook include a rape scene and an image of Sir Thomas sexually involved with a slave woman.

20 Blake's illustrations to Stedman were published in 1796, but he had been working on them for some years.

21 Anne Rubenstein and Camilla Townsend write of "Captain Stedman's political desire to see slavery continue albeit in a gentler form" (273).

22 Austen advises her niece, Anna Austen, to observe these same limitations in her novel, telling her: "let the Portmans go to Ireland, but as you know nothing of the manners there, you had better not go with them" (*Letters* 269).

23 As early as 1860, George Henry Lewes pointed out that "there is nothing superfluous" in Austen's writing (175).

24 Ruth Perry talks of "the changing meaning of the English presence in the West Indies during the last decade of the eighteenth century and the first decade of the nineteenth."

Whereas earlier the British were defending slavery, later they were "resisting Napoleon's attempt to re-enslave" Santo Domingo (233).

25 John Wiltshire notes that the dating of the action of *Mansfield* Park is controversial ("Introduction" xliii) and comments, "I do not believe that Jane Austen meant the reader to recognize that the action took place in a precise year or years. This has critical implications, since it gives more weight to her interest in the internal consistency of the action than its correlation with, or referencing of, external events" ("Introduction" xlv).

26 Peter Knox-Shaw comments, "readers today need to recognize that *Mansfield Park* is consciously set in the post-abolition period, in a world that held the aura of a dawning epoch but which held for many the urgent sense that emancipations still pended [...] Emancipation is the theme closest to the heart of *Mansfield Park*" (179). He quotes at length Austen's brother, Francis, who, when in St. Helena in 1808, noticed with approval the legal restraints that had been placed on the treatment of slaves, confirming (as an eyewitness) the "harshness and despotism which has so justly been attributed to the conduct of the Land-holders, or their managers in the West India Islands." To this Francis adds, "slavery, however it may be modified, is still Slavery" (164). See also Harris 80.

27 Austen's father was a trustee for an Antiguan plantation belonging to James Nibbs, who would become the godfather to Austen's eldest brother, James (Tomalin 289). Perry points out the Austen family's "many connections with the planter class" (236).

28 David Monaghan writes, "in a society based on the cash ethic, those who have managed to accumulate excessive wealth do not commonly employ it" in honourable ways (111). Mary Burgan notes, "Sir Thomas can sacrifice his daughter to the exigencies of family aggrandizement on the basis of family bonds" (546).

29 As Peter Knox-Shaw comments, Sir Thomas in this scene with Fanny becomes "a monster of imperiousness" (188).

30 MacIntyre notes that Fanny's act in refusing Crawford is a matter of doing right "for the sake of a certain kind of happiness and not for utility" (242).

31 The marriage, of course, is also a response to Maria's growing longing for liberty. After Henry Crawford leaves, she feels that "independence was more needful than ever; the want of it at Mansfield more sensibly felt. She was less and less able to endure the restraint which her father imposed. The liberty which his absence had given was now become absolutely necessary" (217).

32 *Pride and Prejudice*, with its ongoing debate about marriage and money, foreshadows *Mansfield Park* in this respect.

33 Peter Knox-Shaw, commenting on Mary's "London maxim," notes that "warnings against the uncurbed mercenary spirit were a feature of Enlightenment writing from the time of Adam Smith, and are amplified by many of the movement's nineteenth century heirs" (195).

34 Jillian Heydt-Stevenson provides a detailed (and rather over-read) account of possible bawdy humour in Austen's novels.

35 Leona Toker notes that the contempt Julia and Maria feel for Fanny because she does not want to learn drawing or music arises from the fact that these accomplishments belong to "the semiotics of 'conspicuous leisure'" (227).

36 In *Sense and Sensibility*, one indication that Edward is a man of principle is his longing for work, a longing that is frustrated by his mother's authoritarianism and his own depressed state.

37 Edward Copeland's rather different – or differently expressed – position, that this is a novel about "disastrous consumer decisions," is based on much the same evidence (*Women Writing* 102).

Chapter Five Speech and Silence in *Emma*

1 Mr Knightley talks to Mrs Weston about Emma (78–82) and makes some observations about Jane Fairfax (302–6). As John Wiltshire observes, the conversation between John Knightley and Jane Fairfax (about walking to the post office) is not told from Emma's point of view (*Body* 115). Mrs Elton complains to her husband about the deficiencies of Emma's wedding (405). I believe that these are the only places in the novel in which we see through other eyes than Emma's.
2 James Thompson writes of the "remarkable sense of community that makes this novel so extraordinary at every point" (167).
3 William Deresiewicz argues for the Longbourne-Meryton community as one of *Pride and Prejudice*'s "principal figures" (503). He goes on to suggest that it is "Austen's most deliberate and sustained critique of community" (504), though most critics would consider *Emma* as even more concerned with community, as I do myself.
4 Austen also draws attention to the significance of the word (in this case the written word) through the word games that are played at Hartfield – Harriet's collection of riddles and the jumbles of letters played with the children's alphabets. Tellingly, Mr Elton composes a pretentious and clichéd riddle and Frank Churchill uses the letter game as a cover for communicating with Jane.
5 James Boyd White argues that Austen "has no notion of a self untouched by its conduct or of a mind or heart divorced from its expressions" (184).
6 Nancy Armstrong comments, "she produces a prose style capable of displaying endless individual variants within polite spoken English" (137).
7 Amy Heckerling's brilliant film, *Clueless*, resembles its source text in its use of idiolects. David Monaghan discusses the idiosyncracies of the Los Angeles teenagers' speech (216).
8 J. F. Burrows, in his discussions of various characters' idiolects, comments at some length on Harriet's in his chapter 5 (107–20). Stout notes that "in *Emma*, in particular, dialogue is the medium of ethical discrimination. By their talk we know that the Eltons are vulgar, morally insensitive people; that Frank Churchill is deficient in conscience and control; that Emma herself is undisciplined" (28).
9 Myra Stokes's section on "manner" is very informative about matters of class and education in relation to speech habits (16–27).
10 Juliet McMaster comments on Austen's various indications of the different kinds of verbal exchanges between people – conversation, talk, chat and so on (*Jane Austen the Novelist* 91). The latest of her series of essays on talk in Austen is "Speaking Fictions: The Genres of Talk in *Sense and Sensibility*" (2011).
11 Despite its uneventful nature, as Margaret Kirkham notes, "the plot of *Emma* is particularly complex" (124).
12 Anne Elliot's visits to Mrs Smith in *Persuasion* are a rather different matter, as Mrs Smith and Anne are of the same social class.
13 Maggie Lane observes that "*Emma* is the Austen novel laden with by far the most references to food, and here they build up to show the interdependence of the village community" ("Food" 267).
14 Julia Prewitt Brown, who describes this scene as "simply a case of unrestrained human hostility," makes a similar point: "it is through resisting these irresistible impulses and

hostilities that people in Austen's society can maintain a tolerably open atmosphere for the individual" (*Jane Austen's Novels* 119).
15 In her introduction to *Emma*, Terry Castle discusses how Austen flatters the reader (x–xv).
16 Thomas Gisborne similarly suggests that women, because of their natural "gay vivacity and quickness of imagination," are likely to have "an unreasonable regard for wit and shining accomplishments" (34). However, he approves of women exercising "wit unstained by any tincture of malevolence" (110). Emma's wit at Box Hill is certainly a little stained with malice, if not malevolence. For more of Gisborne's comments on wit, see also pages 267–8.
17 John Wiltshire sees "an element of aggression" in all the speakers who express their kind concern about Jane's walk in the rain (*Body* 116).
18 J. F. Burrows notes that "without a single clear exception the basis of Mrs Elton's deployment of [first person plural pronouns] is a lust for power and 'status'" (25).
19 John Halperin argues that "almost all of the major characters in *Emma* live in a reality of their own devising" (202).
20 Kristin Flieger Samuelian notes the inaccuracy of Mrs Elton's Italian, which Chapman corrects (254). See also Sutherland 214.
21 Janet Todd uses the expression "non-U" about Mrs Elton in "The Anxiety of Emma" (15). She and I happened to use this phrase on the same day at the same conference (the Jane Austen Society of North America Annual General Meeting, Los Angeles, October 2004).
22 The silences in *Emma* differ from those Angela Leighton discusses in relation to *Sense and Sensibility*. Leighton sees Elinor's silence as the product of "reserve and integrity" and that of Marianne as resulting from "nonconformity and emotional powerlessness" (132). Bharat Tandon believes that the tendency to overemphasize Austen's reading of fiction, especially women's fiction, leads to a "disproportionate emphasis on female reticence as a form of quiescence or quietism" ("Singing the Sofa" 169).
23 Nancy Armstrong discusses Emma's politeness, describing it as "the essential quality of the new aristocrat – so closely akin to charity on the one hand, and to condescension on the other, yet utterly unlike them in the complex of emotion from which it springs" (153).
24 Tellingly, it is the relation between a mother-in-law and a daughter-in-law that Iris Murdoch uses as an example of moral action at work in a difficult relationship in "The Idea of Perfection" (312–36).
25 Terry Castle says, "Knightley is the only person who dares to speak to [Emma] with the freedom and loving candour of an equal" (ix).
26 J. F. Burrows notes that, in terms of language use, "the resemblances between Emma and Mr Knightley and between Anne and Captain Wentworth produce the two highest co-efficients in those novels whereas the differences between Catherine Morland and Henry Tilney produce the second lowest of all the coefficients" (92).
27 Bharat Tandon comments: "Austen ends *Emma*, a work which unsparingly faces up to solipsism and loss, with a marriage that is a perpetual conversation" (161).
28 Jenkyns sees him as "a selfish, idle parasite" (153).
29 John Wiltshire notes the "unobserved dutifulness towards her mother," shown in her slipping away from the ball at the Crown to put her mother to bed ("Comedy" 58), and in *Jane Austen and the Body* he notes her kindness to "Old John Abdy" (140).
30 She is, as Alasdair MacIntyre notes, "*exceptionally* favoured because she is *exceptionally* good" (240 – original emphases).

Chapter Six Dandies and Beauties: The Issue of Good Looks in *Persuasion*

1. James Thompson, however, does note "the extraordinary emphasis placed on looks" and writes of *Persuasion* as Austen's "most visual novel" (99).
2. Margaret Kirkham, for instance, takes this passage as one that Austen would certainly have revised (152). Stuart Tave, however, writes of the narrator's comment on Mrs Musgrove's bulk, "it is an observation of general conduct and not specifically an endorsement that it is fair or reasonable" (261).
3. Walter Benjamin, discussing Baudelaire on the dandy, points out the relation between the dandy's consumerism and British imperialism. The dandy is "a creation of the English who were leaders in world trade" (96).
4. The *Oxford English Dictionary* notes that the word was in use "on the Scottish border in the end of the 18th century." The first recorded use of the word "beau," in the sense of "a man who gives particular attention to dress, mien and social etiquette" is 1687. The first recorded use of the word "macaroni," defined as "an exquisite of a class which arose in England around 1760 and consisted of young men who had travelled and affected the tastes and fashions prevalent in continental society," is 1764. The first recorded use of the word "fop," in the sense of "one who is foolishly attentive to and vain of his appearance, dress, or manner," was 1672–76. This verbal evidence suggests that some aspects of dandyism were not entirely new phenomena in Regency England.
5. Jerome McGann attributes this idea to Albert Camus, but provides no reference.
6. However, Brummell fled from his creditors in 1816 and settled in Caen.
7. James Laver recounts this story as being recorded in the 1842 edition of Captain R. H. Gronow's *Reminiscences* (Laver 21–3).
8. Austen claimed to "hate" the Prince Regent (*Letters* 208).
9. This painting is in the National Portrait Gallery, London.
10. Mary Waldron says, "there are clear structural and narratorial reasons why the time period of the novel is 1806–1814 – the absence and wholesale return of naval officers is necessary to the plot" (146).
11. Roger Sales writes of Sir Walter as "an ageing dandy," but he seems to be using the term in a rather general way (172). He does not discuss the implications of dandyism in this novel.
12. This concern is reflected, for instance, in Sir Walter's comments on Lady Russell's failure to use make-up: "'if she would only wear rouge she would not be afraid of being seen'" (215).
13. As Tytler points out, physiognomy has "a long and illustrious history" (35).
14. I was made aware of this interesting study by John Wiltshire's references to it in *Jane Austen and the Body* (163).
15. "In the late eighteenth century the artistic search to impart definiteness to the changes and indeterminateness of phenomena became acute. Physiognomics attempted to establish a one-to-one correspondence between a person's facial features and his or her concealed mental abilities or invisible spiritual characteristics" (Stafford et al. 216).
16. "The unstated perceptual norm that governs our reaction to patients is predicated on a symmetrical and 'minimalist' conception of beauty. Less is more. Even wins over odd. Homogeneity is better than complexity" (Stafford et al. 214). Inevitably given these criteria aged bodies with their accumulations of wrinkles, scars, discolorations and other markings are aesthetically unacceptable.
17. John Wiltshire, whose discussion of Lavater has a different emphasis from mine, argues that "Lavater is relevant to [*Persuasion*] [...] because of the germ of truth, or of

plausibility his new 'science drew upon: the instinct, at its basis erotic or libidinal, to read health and vigour as virtue, to see handsomeness as integrity" (163).
18. The relation is more complex than Sir Walter might care to consider (or than he might grasp).
19. There was an increase of 2,446 per cent in the number of Botox injections in the USA between 1997 and 2002 (Kuper 32).
20. Margaret Kirkham also comments on the way "the role of women as nurses, or ministers to sickness" is treated in *Persuasion* and *Sanditon* (145).
21. Wendy S. Jones comments on this passage, noting that "it is above all this willingness to get beyond the self that makes Anne morally superior" (120).
22. Anne is also exceptionally responsive to her natural surroundings, as is evident in the walk to Winthrop and the descriptions of Lyme Regis.
23. Elizabeth is "cold and unconcerned" at the news of Anne's engagement (248). Sir Walter greeted the earlier engagement with "great coldness" (26).
24. Many critics have noted the botanical and nutritional falsity of Wentworth's analogy. Markovits, for instance, discusses this flaw in his argument (790).
25. Markovits comments, writing about falls, literal and metaphorical, in Austen, "critics often speak of *Persuasion* as Austen's most autumnal novel, a farewell to the concerns of youth. Yet to believe in a Happy Fall is to put one's faith in the concept of renewal, as Austen undoubtedly does in this story in which our heroine [...] sees 'a second spring of youth and beauty'" (789).

Conclusion

1. Elsewhere as she moves towards a conclusion, Austen occasionally seems to detach her readers from her narratives, reminding them of their engagement in the physical act of reading or hers in the physical act of writing: "Let other pens dwell on guilt and misery," she famously begins the last chapter of *Mansfield Park*. John Wiltshire comments on this beginning as a "not uncommon metatextual gesture" in his edition of *Mansfield Park* (736).
2. Peter Graham provides lists of marriages within the novels (110).
3. Not everyone sees the various conclusions as being "proper resolutions." Cassandra Austen was reported to have doubts about the ending of *Mansfield Park*, though as Jan Fergus notes, these reports are themselves rather dubious (*Jane Austen* 144). Several critics of *Sense and Sensibility* have been unhappy about Marianne's marriage to Colonel Brandon; as Isobel Armstrong observes, "by critics generally he is not looked kindly upon as Marianne's husband" (78). Poovey, for instance, sees Brandon as living in a world of "diminished desires" (189).
4. Elinor's misjudgement over Marianne's illness seems to be the result not so much of lack of attention as relying too much on the apothecary rather than on Mrs Jennings, on the professional male rather than the experienced female.
5. Later, Graham refers to William Blake's insistence in *Jerusalem* that "he who wishes to see a Vision; a perfect Whole / Must see it in its Minute Particulars; Organized," lines that I had considered using as an epigraph for this book (Graham 22: *Jerusalem* Plate 91, 20–21; Erdman 251). The "Minute Particulars" of Austen's work are of course not the concrete details used by later nineteenth-century writers such as Anthony Trollope or Margaret Oliphant to establish verisimilitude in their provincial settings.
6. Byrne comments in some detail on the implications of Austen's advice to her niece for our understanding of the conventions of polite behaviour at the period (299).

7 These letters, which also illustrate Austen's affection for her niece and sense of responsibility for her, date from 10–18 August 1814 and 9–18 September 1814 (*Letters* 267–9, 274–6).
8 Austen had already been checking details about ordination, as is evident from the same letter.
9 It is significant that the closest Austen comes to reproducing an actual event in her fiction is in the early, unfinished *Catharine or the Bower*, which was never published in her lifetime. Here the presumable model for Catharine's friend, Miss Wynne, who is shipped off to India in order to find a husband, is her father's sister "Aunt Hancock" (Tomalin 80).

SELECT BIBLIOGRAPHY

"A Bennet Family Portrait." Dir. Joe Wright. *Pride and Prejudice*. Universal, 2005.
Ackroyd, Peter. *Blake*. London: Sinclair-Stevenson, 1995.
Adams, James Eli. *Dandies and Desert Saints: Styles of Victorian Masculinity*. Ithaca: Cornell University Press, 1995.
Adamson, Jane, Richard Freadman and David Parker, eds. *Renegotiating Ethics in Literature, Philosophy and Theory*. Cambridge: Cambridge University Press, 1998.
Amis, Kingsley. "What Became of Jane Austen." *The Spectator*, 4 Oct. 1957: 33–40.
Anon. Review in The British Critic 41:2 (Feb. 1813). *Pride and Prejudice*. Jane Austen. Ed. Robert P. Irvine. Peterborough, ON: Broadview Press, 2002: 482–3.
Armstrong, Isobel. *Sense and Sensibility*. London: Penguin, 1994.
Armstrong, Nancy. *Desire and Domestic Fiction: A Political History of the Novel*. Oxford: Oxford University Press, 1987.
Austen, Jane. *Catharine and Other Writings*. Ed. Margaret Anne Doody and Douglas Murray. Oxford: Oxford University Press, 1993.
———. *Emma*. Ed. Kristin Flieger Samuelian. Peterborough, ON: Broadview Press, 2004.
———. *Jane Austen's Letters*. Ed. Deirdre Le Faye. Oxford: Oxford University Press, 1997.
———. "Lady Susan." *Later Manuscripts*. Ed. Janet Todd and Linda Bree. Cambridge: Cambridge University Press, 2008: 3–78.
———. *Mansfield Park*. Ed. June Sturrock. Peterborough, ON: Broadview Press, 2005.
———. *Northanger Abbey*. Ed. Claire Grogan. Peterborough, ON: Broadview Press, 1996.
———. *Persuasion*. Ed. Linda Bree. Peterborough, ON: Broadview Press, 1998.
———. *Pride and Prejudice*. Ed. Robert P. Irvine. Peterborough, ON: Broadview Press, 2002.
———. "Sanditon." *Later Manuscripts*. Ed. Janet Todd and Linda Bree. Cambridge: Cambridge University Press, 2008: 137–209.
———. *Sense and Sensibility*. Ed. Kathleen James-Cavan. Peterborough, ON: Broadview Press, 2001.
———. "The Watsons." *Later Manuscripts*. Ed. Janet Todd and Linda Bree. Cambridge: Cambridge University Press, 2008: 79–136.
Benedict, Barbara M. and Deirdre Le Faye, eds. "Introduction." *Northanger Abbey*. Jane Austen. Cambridge: Cambridge University Press, 2006: xxiii–lxi.
Benjamin, Walter. *Charles Baudelaire: A Lyric Poet in the Era of High Capitalism*. London: National Library Board, 1973.
Blake, William. *The Complete Poetry and Prose of William Blake*. Ed. David V. Erdman. New York: Doubleday, 1988.

Booth, Wayne C. *The Company We Keep: An Ethics of Fiction*. Berkeley: University of California Press, 1988.

Bree, Linda, ed. "Introduction." *Persuasion*. Jane Austen. Peterborough, ON: Broadview Press, 1998: 7–37

Brink, Andre. *The Novel: Language and Narrative from Cervantes to Calvino*. New York: New York University Press, 1998.

Brissenden, R. F. "*Mansfield Park*: Freedom and the Family." *Jane Austen: Bicentenary Essays*. Ed. John Halperin. Cambridge: Cambridge University Press, 1975: 156–71.

Bromberg, Pamela S. "Learning to Listen." *Approaches to Teaching Austen's* Emma. Ed. Marcia McClintock Folsom. New York: Modern Language Association, 2004: 127–33.

Brown, Julia Prewitt. "The Everyday of *Emma*." *Approaches to Teaching Austen's* Emma. Ed. Marcia McClintock Folsom. New York: Modern Language Association, 2004: 17–25.

———. "The Feminist Depreciation of Austen." *Novel, A Forum on Fiction* 23 (1990): 303–13.

———. *Jane Austen's Novels: Social Change and Literary Form*. Cambridge, MA: Harvard University Press, 1979.

Brown, Lloyd W. "The Business of Marrying and Mothering." *Jane Austen's Achievement*. Ed. J. McMaster. London: Macmillan, 1976: 44–63.

Brownstein, Rachel M. *Becoming a Heroine: Reading about Women in Novels*. New York: Columbia University Press, 1994.

———. "*Northanger Abbey, Sense and Sensibility, Pride and Prejudice*." *The Cambridge Companion to Jane Austen*. Ed. E. Copeland and J. McMaster. Cambridge: Cambridge University Press 1997: 32–57.

Burgan, Mary. "Mr. Bennet and the Failures of Fatherhood." *Journal of English and Germanic Philology* 74 (1975): 536–52.

Burrows, J. F. *Computation into Criticism: A Study of Jane Austen's Novels and an Experiment in Method*. Oxford: Clarendon, 1987.

Butler, Marilyn. *Jane Austen and the War of Ideas*. Oxford: Clarendon, 1975.

Byrne, Paula. "Manners." *Jane Austen in Context*. Ed. Janet Todd. Cambridge: Cambridge University Press, 2005: 297–305.

Castle, Terry, ed. "Introduction." *Emma*. Jane Austen. Oxford: Oxford University Press, 1995: vii–xxviii.

Copeland, Edward. "Money." *The Cambridge Companion to Jane Austen*. Ed. E. Copeland and J. McMaster. Cambridge: Cambridge University Press, 1997: 131–48.

———. *Women Writing about Money: Women's Fiction in England, 1790–1820*. Cambridge: Cambridge University Press, 1995.

Davis, Kathryn. "Exonerating Mrs Dashwood." *Persuasions: The Jane Austen Journal* 33 (2011): 61–74.

Deresiewicz, William. "Community and Cognition in *Pride and Prejudice*." *English Literary History* 64:2 (1997): 503–35.

Diamond, Cora. "Martha Nussbaum and the Need for Novels." *Renegotiating Ethics in Literature, Philosophy and Theory*. Ed. Jane Adamson, Richard Freadman and David Parker. Cambridge: Cambridge University Press, 1998: 39–64.

Dickens, Charles. *Little Dorrit*. Oxford: Oxford University Press, 1953.

Douglas, Aileen. "Austen's Enclave: Virtue and Modernity." *Romanticism* 5 (1999): 147–61.

Duckworth, Alistair. *The Improvement of the Estate: A Study of Jane Austen's Novels*. Baltimore: Johns Hopkins University Press, 1971.

Dunlap, Barbara. "*Heartsease* and *Mansfield Park*." *Journal of the Charlotte M. Yonge Fellowship* 2 (1997): 1.

Dunn, Judy and Robert Plomin. *Separate Lives: Why Siblings are so Different*. New York: Basic Books, 1990.
Emsley, Sarah. *Jane Austen's Philosophy of the Virtues*. New York: Palgrave Macmillan, 2005.
Farrer, Reginald. "An Anniversary Comment." *Quarterly Review* 228 (1917): 1–30.
Fergus, Jan. *Jane Austen: A Literary Life*. London: Macmillan, 1991.
———. "Sex and Social Life in Jane Austen's Novels." *Jane Austen in a Social Context*. Ed. David Monaghan. London: Macmillan, 1981: 66–85.
Ferguson, Moira. *Subject to Others: British Women Writers and Colonial Slavery, 1670–1834*. New York: Routledge, 1992.
Ford, Susan Allen. "Mrs Dashwood's Insight: Reading Edward Ferrars and *Columella; or The Distressed Anchoret*." *Persuasions: The Jane Austen Journal* 33 (2011): 75–88.
Fordyce, James. *Sermons to Young Women in Two Volumes*. London, 1766.
Fraiman, Susan. *Unbecoming Women: British Writers and the Novel of Development*. New York: Columbia University Press, 1993.
Gard, Roger. *Jane Austen's Novels: The Art of Clarity*. New Haven: Yale University Press, 1992.
Gibbs, Christine. "Absent Fathers: An Examination of Father-Daughter Relationships in Jane Austen Novels." *Persuasions: The Jane Austen Journal* 8 (1986): 45–50.
Gisborne, Thomas. *An Enquiry into the Duties of the Female Sex*. Ed. Gina Luria. New York: Garland, 1974.
Goldberg, S. L. *Agents and Lives: Moral Thinking in Literature*. Cambridge: Cambridge University Press, 1993.
Graham, Peter W. *Jane Austen and Charles Darwin: Naturalists and Novelists*. London: Ashgate, 2008.
Gregory, Dr. *A Father's Legacy to his Daughters: A New Edition*. London, 1784.
Haines, Simon. "Deepening the Self; The Language of Ethics and the Language of Literature." *Renegotiating Ethics in Literature, Philosophy and Theory*. Ed. Jane Adamson, Richard Freadman and David Parker. Cambridge: Cambridge University Press, 1998: 21–38.
Harding, D. W. "Regulated Hatred: An Aspect of the Work of Jane Austen." *Scrutiny* 8 (1940): 346–62.
Harris, Jocelyn. *A Revolution Almost Beyond Expression: Jane Austen's* Persuasion. Newark: University of Delaware Press, 2007.
Heydt-Stevenson, Jillian. *Austen's Unbecoming Conjunctions: Subversive Laughter, Embodied History*. London: Palgrave, 2005.
Horwitz, Barbara. *Jane Austen and the Question of Women's Education*. New York: Peter Lang, 1991.
Hutcheon, Linda. *A Theory of Adaptation*. New York: Routledge, 2006.
Inchbald, Elizabeth. *Lovers' Vows*. In *Mansfield Park*. Jane Austen. Ed. John Wiltshire. Cambridge: Cambridge University Press, 2005: 555–639
Irvine, Robert P. *Jane Austen*. Abingdon: Routledge, 2005.
James, P. D. "Appendix: *Emma* Considered as a Detective Story." *Time to be in Earnest: A Fragment of Autobiography*. Toronto: Vintage Canada, 2001: 243–57.
Jenkyns, Richard. *A Fine Brush on Ivory: An Appreciation of Jane Austen*. Oxford: Oxford University Press, 2004.
Johnson, Claudia L. "Introduction." *Jane Austen's Mansfield Park: A Screenplay*. Patricia Rozema. New York: Talk Miramax Books, 2000: 1–10.
———. *Jane Austen: Women, Politics, and the Novel*. Chicago: University of Chicago Press, 1988.

———. "What Became of Jane Austen." *Persuasions: The Jane Austen Journal* 17 (1995): 59–70.
Johnson, Claudia L. and Susan J. Wolfson. "Introduction." *Pride and Prejudice*. New York: Longman, 2003.
Johnson, Judith Van Sickle. "Austen's Accommodations." *Critical Essays on Jane Austen*. Ed. Laura Mooneyham White. New York: Prentice Hall, 1998: 160–97.
———. "The Bodily Frame: Learning Romance in *Persuasion*." *Nineteenth Century Fiction* (1983): 43–61.
Johnson, Samuel. "The Modern Form of Romances Preferable to the Ancient. The Necessity of Characters Morally Good." *The Rambler* 1:4 (31 March 1750): 27–36.
Jones, Darryl. *Jane Austen*. London: Palgrave Macmillan, 2004.
Jones, Wendy S. *Consensual Fictions: Women, Liberalism, and the English Novel*. Toronto: University of Toronto Press, 2005.
Kaplan, Deborah. *Jane Austen Among Women*. Baltimore: Johns Hopkins University Press, 1994.
King, Amy M. *Bloom: The Botanical Vernacular in the English Novel*. New York: Oxford University Press, 2003.
Kirkham, Margaret. *Jane Austen, Feminism, and Fiction*. London: Athlone Press, 1997.
Knox-Shaw, Peter. *Jane Austen and the Enlightenment*. Cambridge: Cambridge University Press, 2004.
Koppel, Gene. *The Religious Dimensions of Jane Austen's Novels*. Ann Arbor: UMI Research Press, 1988.
Kroeber, Karl. "*Pride and Prejudice*: Fiction's Lasting Novelty." *Jane Austen: Bicentenary Essays*. Ed. John Halperin. Cambridge: Cambridge University Press, 1975: 144–55.
Kuper, Adam. "Life is What You Make It." *Times Literary Supplement*, 2 July 2004: 32.
Lane, Maggie. "The French Bread at Northanger." *Persuasions: The Jane Austen Journal* 20 (1998): 135–45.
———. "Food." *Jane Austen in Context*. Ed. Janet Todd. Cambridge: Cambridge University Press, 2005: 262–8.
Langland, Elizabeth. *Nobody's Angels: Middle-Class Women and Domestic Ideology in Victorian Culture*. Ithaca: Cornell University Press, 1995.
Laver, James. *Dandies*. London: Weidenfeld and Nicolson, 1968.
Leavis, F. R. *The Great Tradition*. London: Chatto and Windus, 1960.
Leavis, Q. D. "'Lady Susan' into *Mansfield Park*." *A Selection from* Scrutiny. Ed. F. R. Leavis. Vol. 2. Cambridge: Cambridge University Press, 1968: 23–64.
Leighton, Angela. "Sense and Silences." *Jane Austen: New Perspectives*. Ed. Janet Todd. New York: Holmes and Meier, 1983: 128–41.
Lewes, G. H. "A Note on Jane Austen's Artistic Economy." *Jane Austen: The Critical Heritage*. Ed. Brian Southam. Vol. 1. London: Routledge, 1968: 175.
Lovibond, Sabina. *Iris Murdoch, Gender and Philosophy*. London: Routledge, 2011.
Lynch, Deidre Shauna. *The Economy of Character: Novels, Market Culture, and the Business of Inner Meaning*. Chicago: University of Chicago Press, 1998.
Macdonald, Susan Peck. "Jane Austen and the Tradition of the Absent Mother." *The Lost Tradition: Mothers and Daughters in Literature*. Ed. Cathy N. Davidson and E. M. Broner. New York: Frederick Ungar, 1980: 58–69.
MacIntyre, Alasdair. *After Virtue: A Study in Moral Theory*. Notre Dame, IN: University of Notre Dame Press, 1984.
Mandal, Anthony. "Language." *Jane Austen in Context*. Ed. Janet Todd. Cambridge: Cambridge University Press, 2005: 23–32.

Marchand, Leslie A. *Byron: A Portrait.* London: Pimlico, 1970.
Markovits, Stefanie. "Jane Austen and the Happy Fall." *Studies in English Literature, 1500–1800* 47 (2007): 779–97.
McGann, Jerome. "The Dandy." *Midway* 10 (1969): 3–18.
McMaster, Juliet. *Jane Austen on Love.* Victoria: University of Victoria Press, 1978.
———. *Jane Austen the Novelist.* London: Macmillan, 1996.
———. "Mrs. Elton and Other Verbal Aggressors." *The Talk in Jane Austen.* Ed. Bruce Stovel and Lynn Weinlos Gregg. Edmonton: University of Alberta Press, 2002: 73–90.
———. "The Secret Languages of *Emma.*" *Persuasions: The Journal of the Jane Austen Society of North America* 15 (1991): 119–31.
———. "Speaking Fictions: The Genres of Talk in *Sense and Sensibility.*" *Persuasions: The Jane Austen Journal* 33 (2011): 172–86.
———. "The Talkers and Listeners of *Mansfield Park.*" *Persuasions: The Journal of the Jane Austen Society of North America* 17 (1995): 77–89.
———. "Talking about Talk in *Pride and Prejudice.*" *Jane Austen's Business.* Ed. Juliet McMaster and Bruce Stovel. New York: St Martin's Press, 1996: 81–94.
McMillan, Dorothy. "Iron Gates and Ha Has: Visible and Invisible Barriers in *Mansfield Park.*" *Austentations: An Occasional Periodical of the Kent Branch of the Jane Austen Society* 10 (2010): 3–18.
Medwin, Thomas. *Conversations of Lord Byron.* London: Henry Colburn, 1824.
Michie, Elsie B. "Austen's Powers: Engaging with Adam Smith on Debates about Wealth and Virtue." *Novel: A Forum on Fiction* 34 (2000): 5–27.
Miles, Robert. *Jane Austen.* Tavistock: Northcote House, 2003.
Moler, Kenneth. *Jane Austen's Art of Allusion.* Lincoln: University of Nebraska Press, 1968.
———. "The Two Voices of Fanny Price." *Jane Austen: Bicentenary Essays.* Ed. John Halperin. Cambridge: Cambridge University Press, 1975: 172–9.
Monaghan, David. "Emma and the Art of Adaptation." *Jane Austen on Screen.* Ed. Gina Macdonald and Andrew F. Macdonald. Cambridge: Cambridge University Press, 2003: 197–227.
More, Hannah. *Coelebs in Search of a Wife.* Bristol: Thoemmes Press, 1995.
———. *Letters to Young Ladies.* New York: Leavitt and Co., 1850.
———. *Slavery, A Poem.* London: T. Cadell, 1788.
———. "The Sorrows of Yamba." *Mansfield Park.* Ed. June Sturrock. Peterborough, ON: Broadview Press, 2001: 497–8
———. *Strictures on the Modern System of Female Education.* London: T. Cadell and W. Davies, 1800.
Murdoch, Iris. "Against Dryness." *Existentialist and Mystics: Writings on Philosophy and Literature.* Ed. Peter Conradi. London: Chatto and Windus, 1997: 287–96.
———. "The Idea of Perfection." *Existentialist and Mystics: Writings on Philosophy and Literature.* Ed. Peter Conradi. London: Chatto and Windus, 1997: 299–336.
———. *Nuns and Soldiers.* London: Chatto and Windus, 1980.
Nardin, Jane. "Children and their Families." *Jane Austen: New Perspectives.* Ed. Janet Todd. New York: Holmes and Meier, 1983: 73–87.
———. "Jane Austen and the Problem of Leisure." *Jane Austen in a Social Context.* Ed. D. Monaghan. London: Macmillan, 1981: 122–42.
———. "Jane Austen, Hannah More, and the Novel of Education." *Persuasions: The Jane Austen Journal* 20 (1998): 15–20.
Nelson, T. G. A. *Children, Parents, And the Rise of the Novel.* Newark: University of Delaware Press, 1995.

Newark, Elizabeth. "Words Not Spoken: Courtship and Seduction in Jane Austen's Novels." *The Talk in Jane Austen*. Ed. Bruce Stovel and Lynn Weinlos Gregg. Edmonton: University of Alberta Press, 2002: 207–24.

Nietzsche, Friedrich. *The Birth of Tragedy out of the Spirit of Music*. London: Penguin, 1993.

Nussbaum, Martha C. *Love's Knowledge: Essays on Philosophy and Literature*. Oxford: Oxford University Press, 1990.

———. "Faint with Secret Knowledge: Love and Vision in Murdoch's *The Black Prince*." *Iris Murdoch, Philosopher: A Collection of Essays*. Ed. Justin Broackes. Oxford: Oxford University Press, 2012: 135–54.

———. *Poetic Justice: The Literary Imagination and Public Life*. Boston: Beacon Press, 1995.

Oliphant, Margaret. "Miss Austen and Miss Mitford" (extract). *Jane Austen: The Critical Heritage*. Vol 1. Ed. Brian Southam. London: Routledge, 1968: 215–25.

Page, Norman. "The Great Tradition Revisited." *Jane Austen's Achievement*. Ed. J. McMaster. London: Macmillan, 1976: 44–63.

Parker, David. *Ethics, Theory and the Novel*. Cambridge: Cambridge University Press, 1994.

———. "Introduction: The Turn to Ethics in the 1990s." *Renegotiating Ethics in Literature, Philosophy and Theory*. Ed. Jane Adamson, Richard Freadman and David Parker. Cambridge: Cambridge University Press, 1998: 1–20.

Perera, Suvendrini. *Reaches of Empire: The English Novel from Edgeworth to Dickens*. New York: Columbia University Press, 1991.

Perry, Ruth. "Jane Austen and British Imperialism." *Monstrous Dreams of Reason: Body, Self, and Other in the Enlightenment*. Ed. Laura J. Rosenthal and Mita Choudbury. Lewisburg: Bucknell University Press, 2002: 231–54.

Plomin, Robert and Denise Daniels. "Why are children in the same family so different from one another." *The Behavioural and Brain Sciences* 10 (1987): 1–16.

Poovey, Mary. *The Proper Lady and the Woman Writer: Ideology as Style in the Works of Mary Wollstonecraft, Mary Shelley and Jane Austen*. Chicago: University of Chicago Press, 1984.

Pride and Prejudice. Dir. Joe Wright. Universal, 2005.

Ragatz, Lowell J. *The Fall of the Planter Class in the British Caribbean, 1763–1833: A Study in Social and Economic History*. New York: Octagon Books, 1963.

Ricks, Christopher. "Jane Austen and the Business of Mothering." *Essays in Appreciation*. Oxford: Clarendon, 1996: 90–113.

Roberts, William. *Memoirs of the Life and Correspondence of Mrs. Hannah More*. London: Seeley and Burnside, 1834.

Rogers, Pat. "Introduction." *Pride and Prejudice*. Jane Austen. Ed. Pat Rogers. Cambridge: Cambridge University Press, 2006: xiii–lxxviii.

Rorty, Richard. "Comment on Castoriadis's 'The End of Philosophy.'" *Salmagundi* 82:3 (1989): 24–30.

———. *Contingency, Irony, and Solidarity*. Cambridge: Cambridge University Press, 1989.

Roulston, Christine. "Discourse, Gender and Gossip: Some Reflections on Bakhtin and *Emma*." *Ambiguous Discourse: Feminist Narratology and British Women Writers*. Ed. Kathy Mezei. Chapel Hill: University of North Carolina Press, 1996: 40–64.

Rozema, Patricia. *Jane Austen's Mansfield Park: A Screenplay*. New York: Talk Miramax Books, 2000.

Rubenstein, Anne, and Camilla Townsend. "Revolted Negroes and the Devilish Principle: William Blake and Conflicting Visions of Boni's Wars in Surinam." *Blake, Politics and History*. Ed. Jackie DiSalvo and G. A. Rosso. New York: Garland, 1998: 273–300.

Said, Edward. "Jane Austen and Empire." *Raymond Williams: Critical Perspectives*. Ed. Terry Eagleton. Boston: Northeastern University Press, 1989: 150–64.

Sales, Roger. *Jane Austen and Representations of Regency England.* London: Routledge, 1994.
Samuelian, Kirsten Flieger, ed. *Emma.* Jane Austen. Peterborough, ON: Broadview Press, 2004.
Scarry, Elaine. *On Beauty and Being Just.* Princeton: Princeton University Press, 1999.
Schaw, Janet. *Journal of a Lady of Quality; Being the Narrative of a Journey from Scotland to the West Indies, North Carolina, and Portugal, in the Years 1774 to 1776.* Ed. E. W. and C. M. Andrews. New Haven: Yale University Press, 1934.
Scott, Walter. Review of *Emma. Jane Austen: The Critical Heritage.* Vol. 1. Ed. Brian Southam. London: Routledge, 1968: 58–69.
Seeber, Barbara K. "A Bennet Utopia: Adapting the Father in *Pride & Prejudice.*" *Persuasions On-Line* 27:2 (2007).
Selwyn, David. *Jane Austen and Children.* London: Continuum, 2010.
Siebers, Tobin. *Morals and Stories.* New York: Columbia University Press, 1992.
Simpson, Richard. Review of *A Memoir of Jane Austen. Jane Austen: The Critical Heritage.* Vol. 1. Ed. Brian Southam. London: Routledge, 1968: 241–65.
Spacks, Patricia Meyer. *Boredom: The Literary History of a State of Mind.* Chicago: University of Chicago Press, 1995.
―――. "Muted Discord: Generational Conflict in Jane Austen." *Jane Austen in a Social Context.* Ed. David Monaghan. London: Macmillan, 1981:159–79.
Spring, David. "Interpreters of Jane Austen's Social World." *Jane Austen: New Perspectives.* Ed. Janet Todd. New York: Holmes and Meier, 1983: 53–72.
Stafford, Barbara M., John La Puma and David L. Schiedermayer. "One Face of Beauty, One Picture of Health: The Hidden Aesthetic of Medical Practice." *The Journal of Medicine and Philosophy* 14 (1989): 213–30.
Stafford, Fiona, ed. "Introduction." *Pride and Prejudice.* Jane Austen. Oxford: Oxford University Press, 2004.
Stedman, J. G. *Narrative of a Five Year's Expedition against the Revolted Negroes of Surinam.* London: J. Johnson and J. Edwards, 1796.
Steiner, George. *After Babel: Aspects of Language and Translation.* Oxford: Oxford University Press, 1992.
Stewart, Maaja. *Domestic Realities and Imperial Fictions: Jane Austen's Novels in Eighteenth-Century Contexts.* Atlanta: Georgia University Press, 1993.
Stokes, Myra. *The Language of Jane Austen: A Study of Some Aspects of her Vocabulary.* London: Macmillan, 1991.
Stout, Janis P. *Strategies of Reticence: Silence and Meaning in the Works of Jane Austen, Willa Cather, Katherine Anne Porter and Joan Didion.* Charlottesville: University of Virginia Press, 1990.
Struever, Nancy S. "The Conversable World: Eighteenth Century Transformations of the Relations of Rhetoric and Truth." *Rhetoric and the Pursuit of Truth: Language Change in the Seventeenth and Eighteenth Centuries.* Ed. Brian Vickers and Nancy S. Struever. Los Angeles: William Andrews Clark Memorial Library, 1985: 79–119.
Sturrock, June. *"Heaven and Home": Charlotte Yonge's Domestic Fiction and the Victorian Debate over Women.* Victoria: University of Victoria Press, 1995.
―――. "Mrs. Bennet's Legacy." *Persuasions On-Line.* 28:2 (2008).
―――. "*Emma* in the 1860s: Austen, Yonge, Oliphant, Eliot." *Women's Writing* 17 (2010): 324–42. Reprinted in *Charlotte Yonge: Rereading Domestic Religious Fiction.* Ed. Tamara Wagner. London: Routledge, 2012.
Sulloway, Alison G. *Jane Austen and the Province of Womanhood.* Philadelphia: University of Pennsylvania Press, 1989.

Sulloway, Frank J. *Born to Rebel: Birth Order, Family Dynamics, and Creative Lives*. New York: Pantheon Books, 1996.
Sutherland, Kathryn. *Jane Austen's Textual Lives from Aeschylus to Bollywood*. Oxford: Oxford University Press, 2005.
Tandon, Bharat. *Jane Austen and the Morality of Conversation*. London: Anthem Press, 2003.
———. "Singing the Sofa: *Mansfield Park* and William Cowper." *Silence, Sublimity and Suppression in the Romantic Period*. Ed. Fiona L. Price and Scott Masson. Lampeter: Edwin Mellen Press, 2002.
Tanner, Tony. "Introduction." *Mansfield Park*. Jane Austen. Ed. Kathryn Sutherland. Harmondsworth: Penguin, 1966.
———. *Jane Austen*. Cambridge, MA: Harvard University Press, 1986.
Tave, Stuart. *Some Words of Jane Austen*. Chicago: University of Chicago Press, 1973.
Taylor, Mary Vaiana. "The Grammar of Conduct: Speech Act Theory and the Education of Emma Woodhouse." *Style* 12 (1978): 357–71.
Terry, Judith. "Sir Thomas Bertram's Business." *Persuasions: The Jane Austen Journal* 16 (1995): 97–105.
Thompson, James. *Between Self and World: The Novels of Jane Austen*. University Park, PA: Pennsylvania State University Press, 1988.
Todd, Janet. "The Anxiety of Emma." *Persuasions: The Jane Austen Journal* 29 (2007): 15–25.
———. *Women's Friendship in Literature*. New York: Columbia, 1980.
Todd, Janet and Linda Bree, eds. "Introduction." *Later Manuscripts of Jane Austen*. Cambridge: Cambridge University Press, 2008: vl–cxxx.
Toker, Leona. "Conspicuous Leisure and Invidious Sexuality in *Mansfield Park*." *Connotations: A Journal for Critical Debate* 11 (2001–02): 222–40.
Tomalin, Claire. *Jane Austen: A Life*. London: Penguin, 1997.
Toner, Anne. "Jane Austen, Frances Sheridan, and the Ha Ha." *Persuasions: The Jane Austen Journal* 32 (2010): 225–31.
Trilling, Lionel. "*Mansfield Park*." *The Opposing Self: Nine Essays in Criticism*. London: Secker and Warburg, 1955: 206–30.
Tytler, Graeme. *Physiognomy in the European Novel: Faces and Fortunes*. Princeton: Princeton University Press, 1982.
Waldron, Mary. *Jane Austen and the Fiction of her Time*. Cambridge: Cambridge University Press, 1999.
Warhol, Robyn. "The Look, the Body, and the Heroine of *Persuasion*: A Feminist Narratalogical View of Jane Austen." *Ambiguous Discourse: Feminist Narratology and British Women Writers*. Ed. Kathy Mezei. Chapel Hill: University of North Carolina Press, 1996: 21–39.
Weil, Simone. *Gravity and Grace*. London: Routledge, 1952.
———. *Waiting on God*. London: Fontana Books, 1959.
Whateley, Richard. Review of *Northanger Abbey* and *Persuasion*. *Jane Austen: The Critical Heritage*. Vol. 1. Ed. Brian Southam. London: Routledge, 1968: 87–105.
White, James Boyd. *When Words Lose their Meaning: Constitutions and Reconstitutions of Language, Character, and Community*. Chicago: University of Chicago Press, 1984.
Wilt, Judith. *Ghosts of the Gothic: Austen, Eliot and Lawrence*. Princeton: Princeton University Press, 1980.
Wiltshire, John. "The Comedy of *Emma*." *Approaches to Teaching Austen's* Emma. New York: Modern Language Association, 2004: 55–60.
———. "Decolonising *Mansfield Park*." *Essays in Criticism* 53 (2003): 303–22.

———. "Introduction." *Mansfield Park*. Jane Austen. Ed. John Wiltshire. Cambridge: Cambridge University Press, 2005: xxv–lxxxiv.

———. *Jane Austen and the Body: The Picture of Health*. Cambridge: Cambridge University Press, 1992.

———. "*Mansfield Park, Emma, Persuasion.*" *The Cambridge Companion to Jane Austen*. Ed. E. Copeland and J. McMaster. Cambridge: Cambridge University Press, 1997: 58–83.

Wollstonecraft, Mary. *A Vindication of the Rights of Woman*. In *The Vindications*. Ed. D. I. Macdonald and Kathleen Scherf. Peterborough, ON: Broadview Press, 1997: 99–343.

Woolf, Virginia. *The Common Reader: First Series*. London: Hogarth Press, 1984.

Yonge, Charlotte Mary. *Heartsease: Or, The Brother's Wife*. London: Macmillan, 1893.

INDEX

(Works by Jane Austen are listed under their individual titles.
Only principal discussions of these works are indexed.)

Adams, James Eli 105
aesthetics, relation to ethics 5
Alexander, Michael 121n19
Amis, Kingsley 122n13
Antigua 72, 75–6, 84, 128n13
Aristotle 3
Armstrong, Isobel 22, 28, 122n19, 123n26, 126n21, 128n14, 133n3
Armstrong, Nancy 75, 93,130n6, 131n23
attention 5–7, 114–15
Austen, Anna 115–17, 128n22
Austen, Cassandra, Mrs (Jane Austen's mother) 125n7
Austen, Cassandra (Jane Austen's sister) 116–17, 119n3, 133n3
Austen, Charles 117
Austen, Edward 117
Austen, Elizabeth 117, 125n10
Austen, Fanny 117
Austen, Francis 117, 129n26
Austen, James 117, 129n27
Austen, Jane: affection for niece 133n7; concern for accurate detail 115–16, 133n5; experience of family life 117, 134n9; juvenilia 115; knowledge of Antigua 129n27; "minimalism" as novelist 75, 115–16; opinions 132n8; religion 62; revision of *S&S* and *P&P* 115–16, 123n1

Barbuda 128n13
Bath 16–18, 49, 102, 106, 110
Baudelaire, Charles 132n3
Belinda (Maria Edgeworth) 1, 16

Benjamin, Walter 132n3
birth order of siblings 123n23
Blake, William 75, 128n19–20, 133n5
bloom 100,106
Book of Common Prayer 126n23
Booth, Wayne 3
Bowen, Elizabeth 11
Box Hill 4, 88, 95
Bree, Linda 102, 110, 125n1
Brink, André 95
British Critic 124n2
Bromberg, Pamela S. 88
Brontë, Charlotte 1
Brown, Julia Prewitt 21, 41, 69, 97, 119n7, 127n1, 130n14
Brownstein, Rachel 27, 122n11
Brummel, George Bryan (Beau) 101–2, 132n6
Brunton, Mary 119n3
Bulwer-Lytton, Edward 101
Burgan, Mary 121n1, 124n15, 126n2, 127n2, 129n28
Burney, Frances 1, 16, 124n6
Burrows, J. F. 17, 72, 85–6, 116, 130n8, 131n18, 131n26
Butler, Marilyn 16–18, 34, 36, 96, 107, 123n25, 124n6, 124n12
Butler, Samuel 11, 121n1
Byrne, Paula 133n6
Byron, George Gordon, Lord 101–2, 108

Camilla (Frances Burney) 1
Carlyle, Thomas 105
Castle, Terry 126n15, 131n15, 131n25

Catharine, or the Bower 119n1, 121n6, 134n9
Cecilia (Frances Burney) 1
Chapman, R. W. 90
Chawton 67
Coelebs in Search of a Wife (Hannah More):
    see More, Hannah
Coleridge, Samuel Taylor 45
comedy 22, 114
community 85, 87, 97–8, 126n16,
    130n2–3
contemporary reception of Austen 1, 87,
    119n8, 122n2
conventions in fiction 24–5, 39, 81
Copeland, Edward 78, 82, 125n9, 130n37
Cowper, William 5, 19, 73
Crabbe, George 19

dandies 101–2, 132n3–4
Darwin, Charles 115, 119n4
Davis, Kathryn 126n19
Deresiewicz, William 130n3
Diamond, Cora 120n17
Dickens, Charles 73, 127n11
Dighton, Richard 101
domestic responsibilities of women 47–8,
    49, 53–4, 55–8, 60–61, 64, 125n9
D'Orsay, Count Alfred 101
Duckworth, Alistair 73
Dunlap, Barbara 74
Dunn, Judy 119n4
dysfunction, familial 15–31, 121n5

Edgeworth, Maria 1, 12, 16, 45, 123n25
education 35–6, 45, 48, 125n10
Eliot, George 1
Emma 33–45, 52–5, 85–98, 112–13
Emsley, Sarah 3, 31, 126n22
endings 111–14, 133n1, 133n3
Erdman, David V. 133n5
ethics and literature 1–8, 116, 119n8,
    120n9–11
Evelina (Frances Burney) 1, 16

Farrer, Reginald 122n13
fathers and father-figures 67–9, 71–3,
    75–9, 86, 97, 100–105
Fergus, Jan 47, 85, 122n19, 123n1, 125n4,
    133n3
Ferguson, Moira 128n18

Fielding, Henry 120n14
film adaptations of Austen's novels 22,
    122n17, 130n7
Fitzgerald, Penelope 11
Ford, Susan Allen 126n19
Fordyce, Rev. James 88

gallantry 90–91
Gard, Roger 25, 119n8, 124n10
Gibbs, Christine 99
Gilbert, Sandra 125n2
Gisborne, Thomas 24–5, 36, 80, 123n21,
    124n6, 131n16
Goldberg, S. L. 2, 120n10
Graham, Peter W. 47, 115, 125n11,
    126n20
Gregory, Dr John 88
Gubar, Susan 125n2

Haines, Simon 5
Halperin, John 131n19
Hamilton, Elizabeth 124n6
Hamlet 15
Hancock, Philadelphia 134n9
Harris, Jocelyn 107, 120n13, 129n26
Heckerling, Amy 130n7
Heydt-Stevenson, Jillian 129n34
Hill, Reginald 15, 121n2
Horwitz, Barbara 124n7
Hume, David 31, 77
Hutcheon, Linda 7, 121n19

improvement (of property) 82–3
Inchbald, Elizabeth 40, 82, 124n6, 127n3
innocence 11
Irvine, Robert 84

James, Henry 11, 120n9
James, P. D. 93
Jenkyns, Richard 127n2, 131n28
Johnson, Claudia 25, 33, 94, 124n5,
    124n14
Johnson, Judith Van Sickle 107
Johnson, Samuel 4, 120n14
Jones, Darryl 126n3
Jones, Wendy S. 123n29, 133n21

Kant, Immanuel 3
Kaplan, Deborah 125n10

INDEX

Kelly, Colonel 101–2, 104
King, Amy 100
Kirkham, Margaret 92, 105, 123n1, 127n5, 130n11, 132n2, 133n20
Knox-Shaw, Peter 25, 36, 77, 90–91, 98, 107, 121n7, 124n9, 129n26, 129n29
Koppel, Gene 124n8
Kroeber, Karl 8, 123n22

La Puma, John 104–5
Lady Susan 47, 125n1, 127n9
Lane, Maggie 125n7, 126n16, 126n24, 130n13
Langland, Elizabeth 125n8
language 92–3, 115, 122n10, 130n4
Lavater, Johan Kaspar 104–105, 132n17
Lavington, Ralph Payne, Lord 76
Leavis, F. R. 3
Leavis, Q. D. 127n9
Lefroy family 117
Leighton, Angela 131n22
Lewes, G. H. 128n23
Lloyd family 117
Locke, John 36, 124n7
"London values" 73, 127n9, 129n33
Lovers' Vows (Elizabeth Inchbald) 40, 82
Lovibond, Sabina 120n15
Lynch, Deidre 127n6

Macartney, George 19
MacIntyre, Alasdair 2, 120n12, 129n30
Malthus, Thomas Robert 124n9
Mandal, Anthony 86
Mansfield Park 33–45, 55–9, 71–84, 112
Markovits, Stefanie 133n24–5
marriage 22–4, 78–81, 111–14, 122n18, 129n32
McGann, Jerome 101, 132n5
McMaster, Juliet 17, 81, 85, 88, 96, 122n10, 122n19, 130n10
McMillan, Dorothy 127n7
Michie, Elsie B. 73, 82
Miles, Robert 3–4, 6, 20, 68, 119n8, 122n15, 123n24
Milton, John 15
Mitford, Mary Russell 121n3
Moggach, Deborah 122n17
Moler, Kenneth 35, 121n8, 123n25, 124n3, 124n6

Monaghan, David 129n28, 130n7
money 60–61, 68, 71–84, 129n32
More, Hannah 2, 4, 15, 37, 48, 76–7, 88: *Coelebs in Search of a Wife* 2, 15, 37, 119n6, 120n13, 124n6, 124n15; sequels to *Coelebs in Search of a Wife* 119n6
mothers and mother-figures 24–5, 47–64, 71, 125n2, 126n15
Murdoch, Iris 3–7, 11, 84, 120n10, 120n15, 131n24
Mysteries of Udolpho (Ann Radcliffe) 12

narcissism 102–5: parental 30, 33, 123n28
Nardin, Jane 72, 119n2, 120n13, 121n9
Newark, Elizabeth 89
Nibbs, James 129n27
Nietzsche, Friedrich 15, 121n1
Northanger Abbey 16–20, 63, 113
novel: as genre 3–4, 74–6, 115–16; Gothic 115; of sentiment 115
Nussbaum, Martha 3–6, 120n9, 120n16

Oedipus 15
Oliphant, Margaret 7, 75, 98, 133n5
Opie, Amelia 12–13, 124n4, 124n6
orphan narratives 1, 12, 119n1, 199n12

over-indulgence, parental 33–45
Parker, David 3, 120n10
Perera, Suvendrini 128n18
Perry, Ruth 128n24
personal appearance 68, 99–110, 132n16
Persuasion 49–52, 99–110, 113
physiognomy 104–5, 132n12–16
Plomin, Robert 119n4
politeness 60–61, 94, 131n23, 133n6
Poovey, Mary 119n4, 133n3
Portsmouth 56–8, 78, 83–4
Pride and Prejudice 21–6, 33–45, 63–4, 111–12, 123n23
prints 101
Proverbs, Book of 59, 86
Proust, Marcel 120n9
pseudogentry 125n6–7

Radcliffe, Ann 1, 12, 19, 69, 121n8
Ragatz, Lowell 76
Repton, Humphry 82

Ricks, Christopher 35, 87
Rogers, Pat 123n1
Rorty, Richard 3, 120n9, 120n17
Royal Navy 103–4, 113
Rozema, Patricia 75, 128n15

Said, Edward 74–5, 84, 128n16
Sales, Roger 132n11
Samuelian, Kristin Flieger 131n20
Sanditon 95, 121n2
Santo Domingo 128–9n24
Scarry, Elaine 5
Schaw, Janet 76
Schiedermayer, David L. 104–5
Scott, Walter 1, 87, 108, 128n17
Seeber, Barbara K. 122n17
self-examination 2, 35–6, 62–3
Selwyn, David 127n2
Sense and Sensibility 26–31, 59–63, 111, 114
Shelley, Mary 45
sibling relations 1, 51–2, 54–5, 57–8, 60–63, 123n23, 125n11
Siebers, Tobin 4, 87, 119n8, 120n11
silence 68, 93–7, 131n22
Simpson, Richard 122n18
slave trade 75
slavery 75–6, 128n18, 129n26: in St Helena 129n26
Smith, Adam 77, 129n33
Spacks, Patricia Meyer 29, 69
speech 17–18, 68, 72, 86–93, 116, 128n18, 130n8, 131n18, 131n26
Spring, David 125n6
Stafford, Barbara M. 104–5
Steadman, Alison 122n17
Stedman, John 75, 128n19, 128n21
Steventon 11, 16
Stewart, Maaja 128n18
Stokes, Myra 130n9
Stout, Janis 124n5, 130n8
Struever, Nancy 31
Sulloway, Alison 93
Sulloway, Frank J. 119n4, 126n13
Surinam 75, 128n19, 128n21

Tandon, Bharat 2, 131n22, 131n27
Tanner, Tony 73, 121n4, 123n28, 126n1
Tave, Stuart 6, 47, 125n5, 126n18, 132n2
Terry, Judith 128n18
Thompson, James 7, 119n4, 127n2, 130n2, 132n1
Todd, Janet 121n4, 125n1, 131n21
Toker, Leona 127n4, 129n35
Tolstoy, Leo 4
Toner, Anne 127n7
Trilling, Lionel 34, 127n4
Trollope, Anthony 133n5
Tytler, Graeme 105, 132n13

Veblen, Thorstein 127n4
Victorian reception of Austen 73–5, 98, 122n18, 127n12, 128n23

Waldron, Mary 4, 15–16, 27–8, 68–9, 107, 119n5, 121n3, 122n14, 123n25, 124n13
Warhol, Robyn 106
Watsons, The 127n6
Weil, Simone 5, 114
West, Jane 123n25, 124n6
West Indies: absentee landlords 76; missionary activity 76
Weymouth 89
Whately, Richard 119n8
White, James Boyd 42, 96, 130n5
Wilberforce, William 76
Wilt, Judith 69
Wiltshire, John 24, 30, 38, 73, 76, 80, 83–4, 103–105, 108, 121n18, 123n1, 125n12, 127n5, 128n18, 129n25, 130n1, 131n17, 132n17
wit 88, 131n16
Wolfson, Susan 25
Wollstonecraft, Mary 36, 45, 48, 57, 91
Woolf, Virginia 105
Wordsworth, William 45
Wright, Joe 22, 122n17

Yonge, Charlotte Mary 7, 73–4, 127n12, 128n1

www.ingramcontent.com/pod-product-compliance
Lightning Source LLC
Chambersburg PA
CBHW021832300426
44114CB00009BA/412